17.95
MEP

OFFICIAL KARATE

David Mitchell is a graduate of the University College of Wales and started the first karate club there in 1964. As well as karate, he has trained in other martial arts. He became secretary of the Welsh Karate Board, chairman of the British Karate Council and, on its inauguration in 1977, first general secretary of the Martial Arts Commission. He serves too on the directing committee of the World Union of Karatedo Organisations and was one of the five members responsible for getting the sport recognized by the International Olympic Committee. In addition he is treasurer of the European Karate Union, is co-opted to the referee councils of the WUKO and EKU, and has become a prime mover in the setting up of the World Karate Medical Congress.

The author has advised the Chinese Wu Shu Federation on the setting up of an international federation. He has also worked closely with the British Taekwondo Board (WTF), the British Ju Jitsu Association and the British Amateur Full Contact Association.

David Mitchell is also the author of *Official WTF Taekwondo*, published by Stanley Paul in the same series.

Also published by Stanley Paul

OFFICIAL WTF TAEKWONDO
David Mitchell

DEFEND YOURSELF WITH KARATE
A P Harrington

THE KARATE-Dō MANUAL
P M V Morris

THE JUDO MANUAL
G Hobbs and T Reay

OFFICIAL KARATE

David Mitchell

**The Martial Arts Commission
of Great Britain**

STANLEY PAUL
London   Melbourne   Auckland   Johannesburg

Copyright © text and illustrations Antler Books Ltd 1986
All rights reserved

First published in 1986 by
Stanley Paul & Co. Ltd

Reprinted 1987 (twice)

An imprint of Century Hutchinson Ltd
Brookmount House, 62–65 Chandos Place,
Covent Garden, London WC2N 4NW

Century Hutchinson Australia (Pty) Ltd
PO Box 496, 16–22 Church Street, Hawthorn,
Melbourne, Victoria 3122

Century Hutchinson New Zealand Limited
32–34 View Road, PO Box 40–086, Glenfield, Auckland 10

Century Hutchinson South Africa (Pty) Ltd
PO Box 337, Bergvlei 2012, South Africa

Photography by Mike O'Neill

Line drawings by MJL Cartographics

Phototypeset in Linotron Sabon
by Input Typesetting Ltd, London

Printed and bound in
Great Britain by Butler and Tanner Ltd, Frome

British Library Cataloguing in Publication Data

Mitchell, David, *1944–*
   Official karate.
   1. Karate
   I. Title   II. Martial Arts Commission
   796.8′153   GV1114.3

ISBN 0 09 163431 8

Contents

Acknowledgements	6
1. The Nature and History of Karate	8
2. The Development of Karate	23
3. The Practice of Karate	33
4. The Stances of Karate	42
5. The Weapons of Karate	52
6. The Blocks of Karate	67
7. Developing Force in Karate	78
8. The Basic Techniques of Karate	84
9. Combination Techniques of Karate	102
10. Karate Katas	112
11. Pre-arranged Sparring	120
12. The Tactics of Free Sparring	131
13. Competition Karate	142
14. Fit to Fight	154
15. Health and Safety in the Dojo	166
16. Japanese Terminology	170
Basic Katas for Practice	176
Index	190

Acknowledgements

I would like to express my sincere thanks to all those who assisted me in the writing of this book. In particular, I would like to thank:

Tony Y. K. Leung for access to information on the Shaolin Temple, which he has researched firsthand.
Jeremy Yau for information on the teachings of Bodhidharma.
Keiji Tomiyama for his patient unravelling of karate's development on Okinawa and in Japan.
Mitsusuke Harada for insights into early Japanese karate practice and the transition of Funakoshi's shorin ryu into modern Shotokan. Thanks also to him for his entertaining lectures on the development of sparring and the organization of the early Japan Karate Association and the Shotokai.
Morihei Higaonna and James Rousseau for information on Goju ryu history and training.
Yasunari Ishimi for his patient description of Shito ryu's origins and his insights into the *do*.
The late Hironori Ohtsuka for a fascinating discussion on Wado ryu karate.
Brian Dowler for information on Masutatsu Oyama and his pragmatic philosophy of karate jutsu.
Doctor David Scott for valuable information on Uechi ryu.
Yoshinao Nanbu for discussing the formation of Sankukai and Nanbudo.
David Donovan, the world's greatest karate coach, for his advice and information on the tactics of free fighting. Also for a description of Ishin ryu.
Tatsuo Shimabuku for a regrettably short interview on the nature of his Isshin ryu karate.
Tommy Morris, the world's leading WUKO referee, for the insight he has given me into the rules; also for his detailed analysis of Shukokai karate and high-energy techniques.
Jon K. Evans of WUKO for a fascinating description of the training methods of Tsutomo Oshima of the Shotokai.
Bernard Creton for his thought-provoking analyses of power development and stances. Also for agreeing to be photographed throughout this book, in association with his senior colleague, Lee Costa.
Ziggy Boban for effectively demonstrating the development of relaxed power in karate.

David Mitchell
London, 1986

CHAPTER 1: THE NATURE AND HISTORY OF KARATE

What is Karate?
Karate is a system of fighting which originated on the island of Okinawa, which lies 450 kilometres southwest of Japan. The term *karate*, meaning 'China hand', first appears in the latter half of the seventeenth century when a famous Master took the name 'Karate Sakugawa'. Sakugawa was a student both of the native Okinawan fighting art of *to-de* and one of the many Chinese martial arts (or *chuan'fa*).

Karate has no single point of origin, though it is principally associated with the Okinawan towns of Shuri (the feudal capital), Tomari and Naha, and also with the Chinese settlement at Toei.

At the end of the eighteenth century, the practice of karate was encouraged and the Okinawan schoolmaster Gichin Funakoshi gave a demonstration in Kyoto. Five years later, he returned to Japan and took up residence there. Other Okinawan Masters followed and, within a short time, the Japanese were producing their own karate teachers.

Modern karate is a well-organized and regulated fighting system using punches, kicks and strikes as its weapons. Over the years, much work has been done on the development of impact force with the result that karate blows can be extremely forceful. A skilled *karateka* (one who practises karate) can shatter several bricks with a single blow. Karate is also a combat sport, utilizing controlled techniques to score points.

Karate's Origins and History

The Shaolin monastery
Early karate development is closely linked with the practice of the Chinese martial arts. These are known under various names, such as *kung fu*, *wushu*, *chuan'fa*, etc. China has a very ancient civilization and no one can say how, when or where its martial arts originated. A great many legends abound and the most famous concerns the Shaolin Temple and the Indian Zen Buddhist monk Bodhidharma (Daruma to the Japanese,

Figure 1 Developing power in karate technique

Ta Mo to the Chinese). He is said to have brought about great development in the study of *wushu* through his teachings at the monastery and is often referred to as the father of kung fu.

Entertaining though this legend is, there is little evidence to support it. The Shaolin monastery still exists at the northern foot of the Sungshan mountain in the northwestern part of T'eng feng district in the Hunan province of southern mainland China. Historical records are unclear about the exact date the monastery was built, though most place it around 496/7 AD, in the Northern Wei Dynasty. The commissioning ruler was Hsiao Wen.

There were, in fact, two Shaolin monasteries, the other located at the foot of the Szu-kai peak of the Pang mountains in Chi district, Hopei province. The records of this monastery show no involvement with wushu.

During the wars between north and south in the sixth century AD, the Sungshan monastery was destroyed by fire. At the turn of the sixth century, in the reign of Emperor Sui Wen-Ti, it was rebuilt and renamed Chi-hu-ssu (Ascending the Hill Monastery). During the Tang Dynasty (AD 618–960), the monastery's name was again changed to Siu Lum (Shaolin).

During this latter period, the monastery gained in importance as a centre for martial art studies. It came to the aid of Li Shih-min (later to become the second Tang Dynasty Emperor, T'ai Tsung) in his battle with the usurper Wang Shih-chung, by supplying the former with fourteen monks trained in the martial arts. These acted as the spearhead of Li's victorious forces. Li was so impressed with their martial ability that he tried to persuade them to become generals in his army. All but one refused and asked leave to continue with their devotions to Buddha in Shaolin. The grateful Emperor granted their wish and awarded each a royal cloak. He also presented the monastery with a tablet, commemorating the monks' valour and skill.

The monastery continued to prosper into the Ming Dynasty (AD 1368–1644). During the sixteenth century, the Shaolin monk Yueh Kung answered Emperor Wan Piao's call to arms and, with thirty fellow monks, went to meet the Japanese invaders in Sungkiang. The monks used iron clubs to great effect, slaying many of the foe. Despite their skill and ferocity, they were overwhelmed and killed by weight of superior numbers.

In 1628, the soldier Mao Yuan-yi offered his manual on quarterstaff fighting to the throne. This long treatise, called *Wu Pei-chih*, covered strategy, tactics, weapons' usage and deployment. The monks did not restrict their martial art to members of the Temple and so it spread throughout China.

With the advent of firearms, the Manchu Emperors and foreign interference, the prestige of the Shaolin monastery declined. During the civil war between Chiang Kai-shek and the warlord Feng in the early twentieth century, parts of the monastery were burned. Fortunately its famous wall murals, showing the monks practising wushu, were unharmed. In 1949, monks were allowed to return to the monastery, but many took up posts in civil administration, introducing wushu into the curriculum of local schools. In 1955, the Commission for Physical Culture began an intense investigation into the roots of wushu and, since then, the Shaolin Temple has been partially renovated.

Bodhidharma

Bodhidharma is venerated as the twenty-eighth reincarnation of Buddha. He came to the Shaolin Temple from India during the Liang Dynasty (AD 502–557) and spent nine years in meditation. Near the monastery are two ancient relics, called the *mien-pi-shih* ('gazing stone') and the *mien-pi-an* ('gazing shrine'). Bodhidharma is claimed to have used both as aids to his Zen meditation.

He is credited with introducing to the monks of Shaolin two sets of exercises called 'washing the marrow' and 'exchanging the sinews'. These were claimed to have martial art connotations. There is, however, little evidence to link Bodhidharma with the initial development of martial arts within the monastery. One legend associates him with teaching the *shi-pa lohan*, or 'eighteen lohan' style of wushu, from which all subsequent forms of Shaolin martial art developed.

Whether or not he was responsible for the development of Shaolin martial art, his name, more than any others, is often linked to it and therefore to karate.

The martial art of the Shaolin Temple

Shaolin martial arts are characterized by their emphasis on breathing and muscle power. They belong to that class of wushu called *wai-chia*, or 'external'. Within wai-chia, there are five basic forms from which have come a multitude of schools and styles. Those which developed in the south of China tended to be less agile, relying upon rigid stances which make the user immovable. Northern Shaolin styles are more open, with greater emphasis on acrobatic skill.

The influence of Chinese martial art in Okinawa

Okinawa lies a mere 550 kilometres due east of the southern Chinese mainland. It is one of a chain of islands known as the Ryukyus which form natural stepping stones between China and Japan. During the seventh century AD, Okinawa received many immigrants from southeast Asia. During the eleventh century, a force of Japanese warriors fleeing from the Taira–Minamoto wars landed there.

In the fourteenth century AD, Okinawa was divided into three independent principalities. These were Hokuzan in the north, Nanzan in the south and Chuzan in the centre. In 1349 Satto, the King of Chuzan, approached China and sought alliance. In 1372 this was granted and, from then on, Chuzan paid tribute every two years. As part of the alliance, in 1393 a large Chinese settlement consisting of thirty-six families came to live in the village called Toei, or Kume Mura. A reciprocal group of Okinawans was permitted to settle on mainland China.

In 1429 King Sho Hashi unified Okinawa's three kingdoms, took Shuri as the nation's capital and increased trade with southeast Asia, Africa and the Indies. His successor, Sho Shin, became alarmed at the military conflicts developing outside of Okinawa and declared a unilateral abolition of weapons. All the nation's arms were collected up and stored under lock and key at Shuri arsenal.

At that time, Japan was ruled by the Tokugawa Shogunate, which remained in power through its skilful playing off of one faction against the other. The Satsuma clan were becoming increasingly militant and, to distract them, the Shogun encouraged their invasion of Okinawa. This took place in February 1609, when a force of 3,000 warriors led by Kabagama Hisataka landed at Matabu peninsula and slaughtered the handicapped Okinawans. A mere two months after landing, the Japanese had overrun Okinawa and set up their occupation headquarters at Shuri Castle.

Despite the invasion, interference with the day-to-day running of the country was minimal and the Chinese village at Kume continued to flourish. In 1661 the Chinese military attaché Kong Shang-Kung (Kushanku to the Okinawans) was sent to Okinawa. He was a meek, scholarly man and an expert in martial art footwork. During his six-year tour of duty, he taught two Okinawans, Karate Sakugawa and Kitan Yari, elements of Shaolin martial art, including the training form called *kwanku*, which means 'a look to heaven'. Sakugawa was already an expert in *to-de* (Okinawan martial art) as taught by Master Takahara and combined these two separate systems in the shurite school.

Other military attachés who made contributions to Okinawa's developing martial art were Iwah, Ason, Waishinzan and Chinto. The latter is remembered today through the karate training form of that name. This employs remnants of classical southern Shaolin techniques and is often called the 'crane on a rock' form.

In 1669 the Satsuma overlords issued an edict that Okinawans must not bear arms. The national sword smithy at Shuri Castle was destroyed and it became a criminal offence for an Okinawan to carry a weapon. This prohibition forced the Okinawan peasantry to rely upon agricultural and domestic tools that could be adapted as covert weapons. Despite the ban on weapons, Okinawans still travelled to China for instruction in wushu. One such person was the grandson of Kitan Yari, Chatan Yari. He spent twenty years on the mainland learning from the Shaolin Master Wong Chung-Yoh.

Okinawa continued to pay its biennial tribute to China up until 1871. In that year, the ship carrying tribute was wrecked on Taiwan and the Japanese government began agitating for tighter control over Okinawa. Until hen, the Satsuma occupation had been entirely unofficial. Later in that same year the Japanese Home Minister visited China and was angered to find Okinawans at the Peking Court. This prompted the Japanese to regularize Okinawa's position and a garrison was established in Naha. Tighter restrictions were imposed and the Japanese took control of the island's police and judiciary.

These harsh measures produced resistance centred around Kume village and there were sporadic outbreaks of rioting involving to-de groups. Some collaborators were beaten up and their property destroyed. The Japanese replied with even harsher controls and the Okinawans responded by burning down the mainland offices of the Ryukyu Trading Company. This was the last straw and, to guarantee the Okinawan people's cooperation, their King, Sho Tai, was taken into protective custody. Travel between Okinawa and China became strictly controlled but, despite this, numbers of Okinawans managed to escape to Fukien.

The three main forms of to-de practised were named after the neighbouring towns of Shuri (*shurite*), Naha (*nahate*) and Tomari (*tomarite*). As the art spread through the country, these distinctions became blurred, with nahate and tomarite combining to form *shorei ryu*. Shurite evolved into *shorin ryu*. The former was a hard style comprised of rigid stances and strong techniques. The latter favoured mobility and faster, less powerful movements.

The Japanese introduced conscription in 1898 but found the Okinawans unenthusiastic in their support. To increase their martial ardour, it was decided to teach them Japanese military arts. The first public display of *karate jutsu* was given by the schoolteacher Gichin Funakoshi.

About this time, the leaders of the Okinawan

Shobukai met in the Nawa Showa Hall and agreed to rename their fighting system karate. This was derived from *kara*, meaning 'China', and *te*, meaning 'hand'. Thus the techniques of China hand were called *karate jutsu*. The term *kempo* was also used, this being an Okinawan reading of the Chinese term *chuan'fa* ('boxing').

The role of Funakoshi in developing karate

Gichin Funakoshi was born in 1868, the year of the Meiji Restoration. His birthplace was the Okinawan capital of Shuri. He was a weak child and took up karate jutsu to improve his health. His teacher was Yasutsune Azato, a Master of shorin ryu karate jutsu whose training lineage could be traced right back to Matsumura, the student of the Chinese military attaché Iwah. Funakoshi was Azato's only pupil and trained under conditions of great secrecy. Training techniques were not written down and were taught by simply copying the teacher's actions. Many had no names and it was left to the student to discover the finer points of their usage.

Funakoshi also trained under Ankoh Itosu, whose training lineage went back to Gasukuma, the latter being a student of the Chinese military attaché Chinto. The Master Matsumura also took a hand in Funakoshi's training and, by the time the latter was only twenty years old, he had secured a wide base of knowledge and competence.

He qualified as a primary schoolteacher and, because of his eloquence and ability, was elected chairman of the Okinawan Shobukai, a body set up to promote the practice of karate jutsu. His wife also practised karate jutsu and became a proficient performer in her own right. Funakoshi was selected by Admiral Rokuro Yashiro to instruct members of the Japanese navy. In 1917 he gave the first public display of karate jutsu, at the Hall of Ancient Virtue in Kyoto, on mainland Japan. In 1921 Crown Prince (later Emperor) Hirohito visited Shuri and witnessed an impressive display by Funakoshi who was, by then, fifty-three years of age.

Also in 1921, Funakoshi resigned as a schoolteacher to teach karate full time. That same year he gave a demonstration at the Womens' Higher School in Ochanomizu, Tokyo, and subsequently called at the Kodokan Institute of Judo where he met the founder of judo, Jigoro Kano. Kano was much taken by ryukyu karate jutsu and persuaded Funakoshi to teach him some basic movements. Funakoshi was equally impressed with the way Kano had refined the brawling art of jiu jitsu into the scientific combat sport of *judo* ('the compliant way').

In 1922 Funakoshi was asked to give a demonstration of karate jutsu at the All-Japan Athletics Exhibition in Tokyo. His book, *Ryukyu Kempo Karate* was also published and became the first training manual. That same year, he came to Japan to live and, at first, found it difficult to make ends meet. He taught at a dilapidated *dojo* (training hall) in Meseijuku and also at universities and military establishments. When things got worse, he earned a little extra money working as a janitor.

During 1933, in response to the increasing anti-Chinese sentiments developing in Japan, Funakoshi changed the meaning of karate from 'hand of China' to 'empty hand'. Just as 'two' and 'too' sound the same but are written differently, so *kara* meaning 'China' became *kara* meaning 'empty'. To honour his contribution to the development of karate jutsu in Japan, a nationwide karate committee set up in 1935 raised sufficient money to build the first-ever karate dojo. This was named Shotokan, *kan* meaning 'club' and *Shoto* being Funakoshi's pen-name. The dojo was destroyed in an air raid during the Second World War.

In 1935, Funakoshi renamed karate jutsu, *karatedo*. Whereas *jutsu* indicated a practical system, *do* meant a way of self-improvement. Funakoshi summed up his philosophy by saying that 'Karatedo strives internally to train the mind to develop a clear conscience, enabling one to face the world truthfully . . . mind and technique are to become one in true karate.'

After the war, the American occupation prohibited judo but failed to understand the nature of karate and allowed it to continue. Funakoshi taught the physical education officer of the US air base at Tachikawa and gave a demonstration for the commander of Kisarazu air base. The other members of his demonstration team included Isao Obata, Toshio Kabata and Masatoshi Nakayama. Funakoshi died in 1957, at the age of eighty-nine. He was succeeded as Chief Instructor to the Shotokan by his student, Masatoshi Nakayama.

The other Okinawan Masters
Kannryo Higaonna is a key figure in the development of two major styles of karate. He was born in 1853 and became apprenticed to the trader Yoshimura. His job involved frequent trips to the Chinese mainland where he came in contact with wushu. He remained in Fukien and trained in the Shaolin arts under the Hung stylist Liu Liang-Hsing, becoming so powerful that he was nicknamed Gyukei, meaning 'bull-like'. His first student was Chojun Miyagi and his second Kenwa Mabuni. Higaonna died in 1915, aged seventy.

Miyagi was born in the city of Naha on 24 April 1888 and trained in Higaonna's nahate from the age of fourteen. Training was arduous and concentrated upon the practice form known as *sanchin*. When Higaonna died in 1915, Miyagi went to China and learned the *nei chia* or 'internal' forms of wushu from Rin Rin Ko. These are quite different from the hard styles of the Shaolin Temple and are believed to stem from Taoist, rather than Buddhist, origins.

Just as there are several forms of external wushu, so there are three basic forms of the internal. The first and simplest is hsing-yi, the intermediate is pa-kua and the most advanced is tai chi. All rely upon the influence of the mind and not upon the muscles. For this reason, the internal forms are often called 'soft', to distinguish them from the hard Shaolin schools.

Miyagi returned to Okinawa in 1917 and opened a dojo in the garden of his house. Despite wind and rain, he continued training and there is a story of him going to the nearby beach to practise his sanchin form against the fury of a typhoon. He named his style of karate *Goju ryu*, *ryu* being a Japanese martial arts word meaning 'school' and *Goju* meaning 'hard/soft'. The hard Shaolin and soft wushu might not appear to be compatible but Miyagi succeeded in effectively combining them to the detriment of neither.

Being much influenced by classical wushu, he did not believe in granting coloured belts as a mark of competence. He believed quite simply that, if a student was good enough, he did not need a black belt to prove it and, if he was not good enough, he wouldn't get one anyway.

As a result of Funakoshi's teachings in Japan, there was a tremendous demand for more instructors and, in 1928, Miyagi accepted a teaching post with Kyoto's Teikoku University. This was followed by visits to Kansai University and Ritsumeikan Daigaku. Despite the opportunities, Miyagi refused to settle in Japan and never spent more than a couple of months there. He continued to train in wushu throughout his life and visited the mainland again in 1936. In 1953, at the age of sixty-five, he died.

His style is continued today through Eiichi Miyasato, Hichiya, Minei, Shinjo, Kanei and Uehara. The best-known international instructor is Morio Higaonna.

Kannryo Higaonna took, as his second student, the Okinawan Kenwa Mabuni. Being a policeman, Mabuni was allowed access to the fighting arts and studied nahate assiduously. Like Funakoshi, he also received instruction in the contrasting shorin ryu from Master Ankoh Itosu. This blending of styles meant that he not only learned the eleven training forms of the naha school but also the forty from the shuri school. Training under tomarite Master Aragaku added a further forty-five training forms, making him the most knowledgeable of all the Okinawan masters.

He became friends with Chojun Miyagi and pretended to be a Goju ryu instructor when they travelled to China for study. He studied southern Shaolin wushu and added even more training forms to his already large repertoire. Not content with this wealth of knowledge, he also studied *nin-jutsu*, 'the techniques of stealth', from Master Saigo Fujita.

He founded the style of *Hanko ryu* which meant 'half-heart school' but later changed this to *Shito ryu*, a play on the names of his two Okinawan instructors. Shito ryu was well received by the other Masters because they respected Mabuni's ability and knowledge. He followed Goju ryu tradition in advising his students to spend some time practising with other styles, so as to deepen their own knowledge of karate. In 1928 Mabuni came to live in Osaka and introduced Shito ryu there.

During his lifetime, the Shito ryu was a unified and strong body but, with his death, many students left to found their own schools. Kuniba developed *Kuniba-shito ryu*, Sakagami founded the *Itosu kai* and Tani, the *Taniha-shito ryu*. The pure line continues through his sons Kenei and Kenzo.

Kanbun Uechi spent thirteen years in Fukien province learning various southern Shaolin forms of wushu. He returned to Okinawa, began farming and got married. At first he did not teach karate but, in 1927, he travelled to Osaka and opened a training hall in Wakiyama prefecture. After twenty years there, he returned to Okinawa and died on 25 November 1948. His son, Kanei Uechi, studied under his father for ten years before opening his own dojo in Osaka. He returned to Okinawa in 1942 and taught at a dojo built for him by his students in Futenma. As with Goju ryu, the basis of *Vechi-ryu* is the training form *sanchin*.

Karate in Japan
Japanese warriors were clad in lacquered wooden armour which made punching or kicking techniques rather pointless. All forms of fighting were restricted to the warrior caste and there was a strict code of military ethics known as *bushido*, 'the way of the warrior'. This frowned upon unarmed combat, regarding it as no more than common brawling. Despite this, techniques were devised to cover the eventuality of a sword breaking or the need to capture rather than kill the opponent. The name of these techniques was *yoroi kumiuchi* (wrestling in armour). Their object was to allow the warrior successfully to close with his opponent and thereby use a short dagger thrust through a weak spot in the armour.

With the restrictions on armed warfare imposed by

the Tokugawa Shogunate, more sophisticated techniques were devised for dealing with unarmed opponents. In the Edo period, schools of unarmed combat known variously as *yawarra*, *tai jutsu* and *jiu jitsu* flourished. There is some evidence to suggest that wushu techniques were adapted for use by the Japanese. These were known collectively as *kempo*.

As the Edo period progressed, so the rule that only warriors could be taught the martial arts was relaxed and many clubs catering for commoners opened. *Jiu jitsu* was supplanted by *kodokan judo* and *aiki-jiu jitsu* by *aikido*. *Atemi jutsu* used the body's vulnerable points as targets for strikes, with follow-up joint locks bringing about the opponent's submission. The purpose of atemi was therefore to distract, rather than to injure. Karate therefore appeared among these as a new and exciting concept.

As it grew in popularity, so the Shotokan set up a grading panel, the purpose of which was to assess the progress of students. They would be examined on their basic techniques, on their pair-form sparring, on their training forms (*kata*) and, later, on their fighting ability. As the classes grew in size, so the method of training changed. It was no longer possible to teach on a one-to-one basis and names had to be devised for techniques which had previously been unnamed. Fortunately, it was easy to break the movements down into their components so large classes could be taught more easily. In jiu jitsu and aikido, the moves are not so easily separated.

Because Funakoshi's original karate jutsu was a fighting art and not a sport, actual combat could not take place since it would have meant the injury of the participants. Funakoshi therefore insisted that kata was the ultimate expression of karate. Younger students were combat-sport oriented and longed to see how their techniques would fare in a sparring situation. At first, pair-form sparring accelerated, with the attacker (*tori*) actually trying to strike the defender (*uke*). Inevitably, this overspilled into unprogrammed or 'free' sparring. To minimize risk, techniques were pulled short of full impact and others were ruled out because of the difficulty in controlling them.

Within the Shotokan, the basic training stances began to lower and greater emphasis was placed upon the development of power through *kime*, or 'focus'. An attempt was made to unify all the various schools of karate into one overall Japanese governing body but this failed. It is only comparatively recently that success has been achieved.

The governing body for karate in Japan is the Federation of All-Japan Karatedo Organizations or 'FAJKO'.

It consists of the four principal associations of karate (*kai*) which are the Gojukai, Shotokan, Shitokai and Wadokai. There are others, but they do not have the same prestige.

The Wadokai was founded by Funakoshi's student Hironori Ohtsuka. Born on 1 June 1892, he began training in jiu jitsu at the age of six. The style practised was shintoi oshinryu, which is an offshoot of *yoshinryu*. At the age of nineteen, he became interested in atemi jutsu and, ten years later, had become the school's leading student. In 1922, he began karate under Funakoshi and soon became an accomplished practitioner. He never forgot his earlier training and began incorporating jiu jitsu principles into his karate. In 1929 he pioneered an early form of karate competition and in 1934 founded his own school of karate which he named *wado ryu*, 'the way of peace'.

The Shotokai were originally members of the Shotokan but left in 1956. They felt that the Shotokan was becoming too preoccupied with non-budo aspects of karate, such as commercialism and sport. They therefore pledged to return to the karate practised by Funakoshi. Their principals included Funakoshi's son Yoshihide, and his senior student, Egami.

The Kyokushinkai was founded by the Korean Masutatsu Oyama. He was born in 1923 and is said to have practised wushu from the age of nine. He came to Japan in 1938 and studied under Funakoshi, achieving his first dan black belt. He subsequently left because he considered Shotokan to be weak and preoccupied with movement in straight lines only. Oyama devised Kyokushinkai karate after spending two and a half years meditating in the mountains. At first he was accompanied by a student, but the student soon left, unable to bear the solitude. *Kyokushinkai* means 'way of ultimate truth'.

The weapons of karate
Okinawan to-de relied heavily upon the use of weapons. Though Funakoshi was an expert with the quarterstaff, the karate he introduced to Japan incorporated little weapon work in the syllabus and, through the years, that which was there has virtually faded out. Weapons' usage is still practised in Okinawa, though it has become a specialized system in its own right, called *ryukyu kobujutsu*, or 'traditional Okinawan martial art techniques'.

Karate was never meant to be an unarmed system. It was a comprehensive fighting art which, because of the prohibition on the carrying of orthodox weapons, relied upon the use of agricultural and domestic tools. Karate did contain a large element of unarmed techniques, but these were only resorted to when a weapon could not for any reason be used. The karate exponent did not learn his art so as to be able to challenge armed professional warriors, for such an action would have been suicidal. Karate simply provided self-defence for use against robbers and brawlers.

The major weapons employed were the *bo* ('quarterstaff'), *sai* ('forked rod'), *nunchaku* ('rice flails'), *tonfa* ('rice grinder handles') and *kama* ('sickle'). Earlier Okinawan traditional weapons such as the *timbei* ('round shield'), *rochin* ('short spear'), *suruchin* ('weighted chain') and *tekko* ('knuckledusters') were not used.

The quarterstaff was known by its full name of *roku-shakubo*, or 'six-foot staff'. It has been used in the combat systems of most countries at some time or another and probably ranks alongside the stone as man's first weapon.

The Okinawan staff is a six-foot length of smoothed oak, with tapering ends. It is circular in cross-section and extremely heavy. Its length is governed by the ease with which it can be wielded by the average person. It must have enough mass to be capable of inflicting injury and yet be light enough to be moved quickly. It is not an indoor weapon because of the space needed to use it properly. Its ends were tapered so the force they transmitted into the target was maximized over the smallest area and thereby rendered more effective. The staff was smooth to make it comfortable to handle and also to prevent it from being easily grasped by the opponent.

In use, it formed an extension of the body, allowing the user to attack effectively while remaining outside the range of a counter. It also reinforced the forearm, allowing hard blows to be blocked without injury. It was seldom swung through the air but merely duplicated the movements of the user's limbs.

Training forms were devised to illustrate and teach its use, the two most famous being *Sakugawa-no-kon* and *Sueyoshi-no-kon*. The first was originated by Karate Sakugawa and the second by Funakoshi's contemporary Master Sueyoshi.

The *sai* is a three-tined metal fork with a weighted handle. It is made of metal and has a round or octagonal section. The origin of the sai is not known, though similar weapons occur in southern China and Indonesia. The sai is generally used in pairs and follows the arm movements very closely. It can be used to stab since the long middle tine has a piercing tip. It can also be used as a truncheon by simply swinging it around and grasping the central tine. When aligned along the forearm, it can ward off blows. Although not weighted for it, the sai can be thrown, and one training form teaches how to do this. Sai were issued to elite units of the Okinawan police prior to 1870. Each policeman carried three, in case one was lost during a struggle.

A variation of the sai is the *manji-no-sai*. This has one of the side tines reversed and the central tine pointed at both ends. The training form for the manji-no-sai is known as *jigen*.

The sickle or *kama* is made from a hard wood truncheon from the end of which a curved knife extends at right angles. The knife is sharpened on the inside edge. Sickles are used in pairs and lend themselves to a variety of offensive and defensive moves. They can be used individually or together, to chop at or snare the opponent. The truncheon can augment a forearm block. They are either held by the handles in the orthodox way or along the forearm with the blades protruding outwards. The training form for the kama is known as *hama-hige*.

The *tonfa* are also used in pairs. They consist of a flattened baton with a peg protruding at right angles near to one end. Originally they fitted into stone grind wheels to turn them. In action, they are normally held by the peg, with the baton lying along the arm. The butt of the baton protrudes beyond the peg and this can be used as a short extension to the fist. Swinging the baton by the peg swivels the longer part forwards, thus increasing its range still further. The swing turns the heavy wooden baton into a cudgel and, when lying against the arm, good protection is given for blocking techniques. There are several training forms for the tonfa, one of which is *yara-sho*.

As its name implies, the rice flail was used to flail rice. Adapted rice flails consist of two heavy wood batons of round or octagonal section, linked at their ends by a thong or length of chain. While the length of baton is fairly constant at fourteen inches or so, the linkage varies according to the preference of the user. A longer thong makes the arc of the free baton much larger and, consequently, slower. Flails with a long link chain were used as garrottes.

If both batons are held, the flail can be used as a truncheon. If one baton is released and swung in a series of figure-of-eights, it can form an effective barrier. The free baton can be caught in flight and the held one released, so that the weapon is quickly switched from hand to hand without interrupting its swings. When used to lash out at an opponent, the range is considerable and the heavy baton packs a lethal impact. There are no set training forms for the rice flail but many have been made up to illustrate its use and to promote timing and dexterity.

CHAPTER 2: THE DEVELOPMENT OF KARATE

The Difference between Karatedo and Karate Jutsu

The Okinawan originators of karate regarded their fighting system as just that: a collection of effective techniques which allowed the *karateka* (one who practises karate) to defend himself. The term *karate-jutsu* merely meant 'techniques of karate'. Each technique was included because it was known to work. When those techniques were introduced to Japan in the early twentieth century, they underwent a subtle change and became karatedo – a 'path', or 'way'. This change was inevitable if karate was to be absorbed within the Japanese culture, a culture rich in military tradition.

The martial art techniques of Japan – *bujutsu* – were the province of only the warrior caste and consequently became associated with a rigid code of honour and discipline. The Tokugawa Shogunate was founded in 1603 and gradually established complete control over the land by systematically undermining and restricting the feudal barons (*daimyo*). It was hostile to the development of military skills and sought to sublimate aggression through elaborate rituals and diversions. The period of the Tokugawa Shogunate, or Edo period, was one of peace and military stagnation.

The backbone of the pre-Edo warrior was Zen. This was brought into Japan during the sixth century AD from China and became widely adopted by the pragmatic Japanese. It worshipped no godhead and concentrated instead upon self-reliance. It called for the warrior to control his own mind and thus achieve a virtuous state which included indifference to death and obedience to superiors.

Zen is derived from the Sanskrit *dhyana* and merely means 'meditation'. The object of meditation is to still the mind and eliminate the ego. The ego is the centre of pride and ambition, both of which can hinder the development of true self-awareness. With the removal of the ego, the mind becomes clear and able directly to experience reality. The person able to eliminate ego is said to have achieved enlightenment (*satori*).

The ego constantly tries to translate reality into definable concepts, just as we use language as a clumsy tool to communicate abstracts. How, for example, does

Figure 2 Pair form sparring

our limited vocabulary cope with the task of explaining colour to one who is blind from birth? When ego is removed and satori obtained, there is no longer a filter between the viewer and perception of the world. The open mind perceives the world directly and without the need for obscuring translation.

When someone inadvertently puts their hand on a hot surface, they do not consciously think 'Ouch – that's hot!'. Their hand is already well away before such a thought intrudes. The body has directly experienced the unpleasant reality of the hot surface and responded in a way involving no conscious evaluation.

Two different schools of Zen exist, one called Rinzai and the other Soto. Rinzai Zen was introduced to Japan during the late twelfth century by the priest Eisai. Soto Zen appeared forty years later having been introduced by another priest, named Dogen. The schools differed in the way they taught the disciple to seek enlightenment. Rinzai tries to do so by posing unanswerable questions that trap the intellect into a conundrum, forcing it to make the quantum jump to satori. Soto sets out to achieve enlightenment by meditation alone.

The Zen warrior ethic was not compatible with the policies of the Shogunate and so the study of milder Chinese philosophies was encouraged. Despite this, it remained firmly rooted and found common ground with some of the Chinese philosophy. Taoism was interpreted by the pragmatic Japanese as a path or way to follow through life (*do*). By cultivating that path, the follower's moral character would improve and society benefit. Any activity could be transformed into a path as long as it involved personal commitment.

The theory behind the *do* was that it was necessary to rise above mere technique. The person who became preoccupied in practising a technique for its own sake would never be other than a technician. His mind would remain fixated upon the technique and therefore diverted from its purpose. Thus, if the technician were attacked, he would contemplate the technique needed to counter attack. His mind would not be relaxed and ready to respond, but rather narrowed down and concentrated upon the matter at hand. In contrast, the master of the way, having transcended technique, was able to act without hesitation and reservation.

In transcending technique, the master of the way had presumably absorbed it, so it became almost like a conditioned reflex – ready to act without interference from the intellect; he would not need to trouble himself about which technique to employ where and when. His mind is divorced from the body's actions. With this mastery comes tranquility; an indifference to life or death.

Practice in the *do* leads to an increase in the mind's powers of unfocused perception. The physical eyes 'see' the opponent who stands menacing in front and the mind perceives his intentions.

As the Edo period progressed and the opportunities for combat diminished, a study of the martial art paths came to supplant that of the techniques themselves. The exponent of *kyujutsu* (techniques of archery) was no longer afforded the opportunity to shoot someone down with an arrow, so he used those same techniques to shoot down his own ego. Thus kyujutsu became *kyudo*, 'the way of the archer'. Although arriving much later on the scene, karate jutsu was not immune to this change in emphasis and became *karatedo*, 'the way of the empty hand'.

In making the change, Funakoshi may have been influenced by Jigoro Kano who had done exactly the same with kodokan judo. The adoption of a Zen-based ethic meant that karate no longer regarded the defeat of an opponent as its *raison d'être*. Although the very name 'empty hand' appears in the first instance to mean simply that karate is a self-defence system involving no weapons, it was actually coined by Funakoshi to try and convey the concept of the Zen mind – that which is empty of ego.

Karatedo was therefore studied in Japan as one of many paths leading to betterment of one's moral character. Modern-day students are advised not to try the converse – which is studying Zen to improve karate. Setting out to attain a coloured belt is motivated by ego and therefore must be avoided. The practice of Zen teaches the karateka that the striving of one fighter against another must not degenerate into a tussle over who is the more dominant (egotistical). The object instead is to strive against oneself and to win, even though the opponent may be awarded the victor's trophy.

Meditation does not require the karateka to sit in lotus position and repeat a mantra. It is perfectly possible during normal training. The mind should relax and not seek to influence what the body is doing. Thoughts of the bank balance and everyday problems should not intrude because they are irrelevant to the here and now being experienced in the dojo. (The kamikaze pilot presumably did not worry overly much about whether he had left the gas on before taking off!)

The here and now is the essential part of our lives. The past is irretrievably lost and the future remains unattainable until the day we die. Therefore, when you are attacked, do not think how nice the flowers look; deal with the attack first, then go on to contemplate other things.

Westerners find great difficulty in embracing the concepts of Zen and therefore a true study of karatedo is denied them. At best they can become masters of karate technique, which is a very poor second. It has been claimed that to fully understand karatedo, you must become Japanese!

As a final comment to this background of karatedo, the student is warned against actively seeking satori. The harder he searches, the less likely it is to be discovered.

The Ryu of Karate

The term *ryu* can be loosely translated as 'school'. It reflects a core of study and tradition, often going back over generations to a divine intervention (*tenshin sho*). The founders of ryu were all leading martial artists who experienced an insight or new understanding that allowed them to revise what they themselves had learned, producing something new and better from it. The element of tradition within the ryu is great and even modern-day masters teach the art in its pure form. The classical ryu permits no variation not set down by the founder and deviations always lead to breakaways from it.

Senior students sometimes find themselves at odds with the leader of their ryu. When this happens and a resolution is not possible, the student may decide to leave the ryu and establish his own following. If he is modest enough to realize that he lacks the ability to found his own ryu and, further, that there has been no flash of divine inspiration to lead him into making such a move, then he is left without direction and must persevere with the training he previously received, teaching it in turn to his followers. This sad situation occurs all too frequently in karate and is responsible for the breaking up of traditional ryu into dozens of parallel associations of clubs and students. In some cases, the degree of splintering has advanced so far that there more people practising a certain style outside that style's ryu than are within.

Goju ryu

Goju ryu means 'hard/soft school'. It was originated by Chojun Miyagi and reflects a blending of the hard Shaolin systems with the soft internal systems of Chinese martial art. There are actually two forms of Goju ryu, one being the product of earlier studies, and the other a result of further deliberation and practice.

When Miyagi went to Japan in 1928, he taught a student by the name of Gogen Yamaguchi. At that time his style was hard and unflinching. As a result of a later study trip to the Chinese mainland, he subsequently modified his approach and changed the practice of Goju ryu. Yamaguchi did not follow suit and continued training in the old methods. Nevertheless, he went on to become a respected and world-famous Master in his own right. This division has since healed and Yamaguchi's sons have now become associated with Okinawan Goju.

Goju ryu is at its best in a close-range confrontation. The stances used are high, and the cat stance (*nekoashi*) is commonly used. Body conditioning plays a greater role in Goju ryu than in other ryu. Training aids to develop strength include the *kame*, or 'stone-filled jar', the *shi'ishi*, or 'strength stones', the *tan*, or 'barbell', and the *kongoken*, or 'iron ring'. The kame is used to increase the power of the grasp and users grip its rolled neck with their fingers and lift it. Regular use builds up the muscles in the forearms, producing a strong grip.

The shi'ishi resemble large lollipops, except that the head is made of stone and is very heavy. The karateka holds them by the shaft and swings them over the head and from side to side, mimicking the action of blocks and counters. This lending of extra weight to the techniques builds the muscles involved in their execution and leads to great power.

The tan is a common training aid in the Shaolin kung fu schools. It is a long barbell that can be rolled down the forearms, stopped by the wrists and then flung into the air, only to be caught and rolled again. This constant hammering against the arms makes them insensitive to pain. The *makiwara*, or punching post, is extensively used as a means of developing focus or force in a strike (*kime*).

Kakete is another vestige of Shaolin practice found in Goju ryu. To perform it, two karateka face each other and bring their forearms into contact. Using hooking movements of the wrists, the arms are alternately pushed out and drawn back against the other's resistance. This can go on for up to an hour and ends with one karateka being finally unbalanced.

There are twelve training forms, or *kata*, within the Goju ryu syllabus. *Sanchin* is one which is used to develop strength. During sanchin, the body is tensed and the hips thrust up and forwards. The student's composure is tested by means of hard blows to the limbs and body delivered by the teacher's hands and feet. The kata *tensho* is used to develop softness and is only taught once the principles of hardness are understood by the student. This kata was specially devised by Miyagi to explain the principle of yielding to the attacker's force.

Other katas used are the two *gekisai, saifa, seiyunchin, shisochin, sanseriu, seisan, seipai, kururunfa* and *suparimpei*. The gekisai katas were also originated by Miyagi but all the rest come from nahate. Accompanying the study of kata, Goju ryu students learn *kata bunkai*. This is an analysis of the techniques used in the kata and serves to explain their purpose.

Goju ryu does not involve itself with competition since it regards sport as incompatible with true karate. In competition, safeguards have to be employed and techniques modified to minimize the risk of injury. Practising competition karate involves the study of a specialized and restricted form of the art which is not integral to its traditional purpose. Therefore, to test techniques, it is necessary to participate in pre-arranged sparring, where one karateka knows exactly what the other is going to do.

The introduction of a grading system into Goju ryu is a comparatively recent innovation.

Wado ryu

Wado ryu, 'the school of peace', could hardly be more different from Goju ryu. It is a typical karatedo ryu founded by the traditional *budoka* (one who practises *budo* – the martial art ways of Japan) Hironori Ohtsuka. The style is light and fast, using evasion and deflection rather than relying upon brute strength. The follower of Wado ryu would say that, if strength is matched against strength, the greater will prevail; it is therefore better to use an opponent's strength to his disadvantage.

As a result of Ohtsuka's skill in jiu jitsu, Wado ryu includes a few throws and locks. Such techniques are rare in karate. Ohtsuka's jiu jitsu taught him to move with an attack, drawing it out and using its very energy to defeat it. To illustrate these principles, Ohtsuka developed what he called *kihon kumite*. This is a form of pre-arranged pair-form sparring involving short, high-level movements and sophisticated evasions.

Typically, Wado ryu stances are high, lending themselves to rapid movements. Energy is developed in strikes through a whip-lash action in which a technique is driven out hard and then snapped back. By comparison with other styles, moves are short and crisp, with blows travelling a relatively short distance. The hips are used to generate power and a strong hip-twist is a feature of Wado ryu techniques. There is no body conditioning and the only training aids widely used are weighted boots, called *geta*. These are strapped to the feet and used to load the legs during kicking exercises.

The katas practised are based upon those used in Funakoshi's Shotokan, a style which influenced Wado ryu to a great extent. Many of the Shotokan katas are, however, omitted and, curiously, Ohtsuka changed many of the names, selecting older Chinese titles for them. Thus the *heian* katas of Shotokan became the pinans of Wado ryu. *Tekki* became *nai hanchi*, *kanku* changed to *ku* shanku and *gankaku* was renamed *chinto*. Other changes were *seishan* (changed from *hungetsu*), *wanchu* (*enpi*) and *passai* (*bassai* dai).

In keeping with Ohtsuka's view of Wado ryu as a way, rather than a collection of techniques, it is heavily committed to competition. Ohtsuka was one of the pioneers of sport karate and organized the first match in 1936.

Shito ryu

Shito ryu is notable for the number of katas in its syllabus. This came about through Mabuni's study of other styles. He not only became expert in those of the naha (shorei) school but also in those from the shuri (shorin) schools, making a total of more than seventy. This deep and abiding interest in kata throughout the ryu has been responsible for some remarkable successes in competition.

Although the style is Okinawan in origin, it has embraced the Japanese principles and become interested in competition. Stances are of medium height, having neither the length of Shotokan, nor the shortness of Wado ryu. Like Wado ryu, the movements of Shito ryu are concise and powerful, avoiding large sweeping techniques which can be seen and easily avoided. One of its most interesting variants is the school of Taniha Shitoryu (synonym = *Shukokai*, or way for all) which was devised by Mabuni's student Chojiro Tani.

Much development work has been done in this school by Shigeru Kimura. He is particularly interested in the development of high-energy strikes and his work has produced some interesting findings. His basic stance is held under tension and, during punch delivery, weight is transferred onto the front leg. A coordination of hip rotation, delayed release spinal torsion and shoulder follow-through produces some quite remarkable impacts on the punching pad. The latter has been developed by Taniha Shitoryu as a means of testing impacts.

The makiwara punching post does not simulate the response of a human body when struck by a technique. When the pad (made from several layers of closed cell foam) is held by a student, a true impression of impact can be safely gained.

Taniha Shitoryu karateka have shown that, for maximum impact, the body must be moving behind the blow as it is delivered. By this means, recoil is avoided and all the power delivered into the target.

Uechi ryu

Uechi ryu is a pure Okinawan school of karate which has been heavily influenced by southern Shaolin martial arts. It uses strikes which are not found in other schools, such as *boshiken*, where the thumb is folded into the palm and the thumb knuckle used to attack a target. *Shoken* is a one-knuckle strike using the index finger. This unusual technique is also found in southern praying mantis wushu. *Yon-honnikite* is a strike made by the extended four fingers to the opponent's vital points. The front kick uses the toes to deliver impact, a method requiring prolonged training before it can be employed with confidence.

The style involves body conditioning and this takes the form of continuous blows to the arms and legs until they lose their sensitivity to pain. Thereafter the student is able to block techniques strongly and without pain. A cornerstone of the ryu is the kata *sanchin* and, as in Goju ryu, the student is tested for weakness during its performance. Sanchin stance and horseriding stance are the only two taught in the style. Other katas in the syllabus are *kanshiwa, seisan, seichin, seiriu, konchin* and *sanseiriu*.

Uechi ryu also teaches the analysis of moves used in kata by means of kata bunkai. Moves taken from the kata also feature in a curious form of training known as *chukan hojoundo*, where they are used as basic self-defence techniques.

Shotokan

Shotokan is the first of the Japanese karatedo ryu, formulated by Gichin Funakoshi from his blending of the styles of Masters Azato and Itosu. The new style was quite different from its predecessors and, as it evolved, its stances became lower and longer and greater emphasis was placed upon the generation of power in striking techniques. The movements are linear, that is to say, performed in straight lines by moving either forwards or backwards. They were originally circular, but as a result of fast attacks in pre-arranged pair-form sparring, the quicker straight steps were substituted.

Shotokan techniques use a conspicuous pull-through in their operation. 'Pull-through' describes the action of pulling back one extended arm in order to power the extension of the other. Thus, in preparation for right head block, it is the left arm which is first fully extended upwards. As it is rapidly pulled back, the blocking right arm rises to meet the attacking technique. The use of pull-through invariably leads to large, powerful movements.

Shotokan kata are extremely numerous, being second in number only to those of the Shito ryu. In some cases, there is more than one version of a kata. Although based upon the lighter and faster shorin ryu, Shotokan's movements are surprisingly robust, and nowhere is this more evident than in the katas which are generally performed with great power and deliberation.

Funakoshi was not in favour of competition or sparring and regarded kata as the ultimate expression of Shotokan. Nevertheless, the younger men of the ryu felt inclined to pit themselves against one another and started to do so through the medium of pre-arranged sparring. Each would take it in turns to attack the other, mustering as much speed, power and determination as possible. As skill developed and techniques adapted, so the first forms of free sparring (*ji yu kumite*) came into being. As the Shotokan increased in size, it became necessary to set up grading panels to evaluate students' performances. These included an examination based upon free sparring.

The Shotokan was instrumental in the development of early karate competition and developed the *shobu ippon*, or 'one ippon', competition system. An ippon is regarded as a definitive strike; one which, if allowed to hit the target with force, would result in the opponent's demise. Shobu ippon competition is still used within the Shotokan.

Shotokai

The Shotokai broke away from the Shotokan in 1956. They considered that, by involving itself with commercialism and competition, the Shotokan was no longer practising true karatedo as expounded by the founder. They therefore set up their own organization and returned to more traditional methods.

The Shotokai do not use obvious force in the development of their techniques. There is less reliance upon the focusing of a technique's power to a fixed point on, or in, the attacker's body (*kime*). In consequence, at the moment of impact, Shotokai students remain relaxed. The front punch is delivered with the lower finger joints protruding, yet still manages to convey considerable penetration and impact. During punches, the elbow joints are not locked. The katas are the same as those in Shotokan but they are practised more fluidly.

The casual onlooker can be deceived by the apparent softness of the movements but, where sparring has occurred between members of the Shotokai and other ryu, the latter have always come off worse. This is probably because of the high degree of awareness training that forms the backbone of Shotokai. The latter appear to have an extra sense which enables them to divine their opponent's intentions and react to them even as they begin.

Kyokushinkai

The Kyokushinkai of Masutatsu Oyama is renowned for its great power. The title of the ryu means 'way of ultimate truth' and adequately describes the underlying philosophy. Kyokishinkai is not a *do* form of karate. It is dedicated to the ability to defend oneself against others and this aim is reflected in the hard and unrelenting training.

In search of a means of testing the effectiveness of the system, Oyama has devised a system of fighting known as 'knock-down', where full power body blows and head kicks can be used. The face is a prohibited area, as is the groin. The bout terminates when one of the fighters has been knocked to the floor. The power of blows is tested by trying them against blocks of wood. Kyokushinkai is the only major style of karate to do this.

Sankukai and Nanbudo

There are many minor karate ryu in existence, some of which are unknown outside of their memberships. *Sankukai* is a small ryu founded by Yoshinao Nanbu (born 1943). Nanbu was a gifted student of Taniha Shito ryu (synonym = Shukokai) and won the All-Japan Student Championships three times. He became dissatisfied with competition karate and practised other major styles. Finding nothing to his liking, he founded the Sankukai.

This is based upon circular techniques and has its own repertoire of katas devised by Nanbu himself. Since setting up the style, Nanbu has developed an alternative and more advanced form, which he calls *nanbudo*.

Ishin ryu

There are two forms of Ishin ryu, meaning 'of one mind', practised today, neither of which bears any relation to the other. The first to receive that name is the style founded by Tatsuo Shimabuku in 1947. Shimabuku was the principal student of the Goju ryu Master Chokei Motobu. He also studied Kobayashi ryu under Chotoku Kyan and blended the two styles into Ishin ryu. Ishin ryu is extremely popular in the USA.

The second style of that name was founded by David Donovan and results from a blending of Wado ryu, Kyokushinkai and Shotokan. Mr Donovan's school is well known because of the success of its students in both the kumite and kata events of international competition. Mr Donovan appears to be the first karate sensei to have analysed the requirements of successful competition and set up a training programme to develop them.

CHAPTER 3: THE PRACTICE OF KARATE

Etiquette and Meditation

The involvement of metaphysical principles within the framework of karate means that there is a certain ritual to its practice. The training venue is known as the *dojo*, or 'place of the way'. It is where the physical techniques and the mental discipline are brought together to produce the whole. The classical dojo is unpretentious and clean, being devoid of murals, pictures and other distractions. Typically in Japan, it is unheated, so the inside temperature approximates to that outside. The floor is highly polished sprung wood.

Since the purpose of karate is to create a better character, the standard of practice in the dojo must be at the highest level. It is unimportant where that dojo is, or what grade the teacher aspires to. The principle remains the same. On a practical level, karate involves the study of techniques which, by their very nature, are potentially harmful to others. The karateka therefore owes it to his fellows to show social responsibility and restraint.

It is said that karate training begins and ends with courtesy and so, on entering the dojo, the karateka hesitates at the threshold and stands with heels together, hands flat on thighs. If a senior person is already inside, the student will face him and perform a standing bow or *rei* (**figure 3**). This is performed slowly and deliberately, with a hesitation when the head has reached the lowest point. It should not be so low that the student cannot keep his eyes upon the senior. If no one is in the dojo, then the bow is towards its centre, or towards any object of veneration that may be inside. Having performed this office, the student is then free to enter in. Each time the karateka enters or leaves the dojo, he must hesitate and perform the standing bow. It should never be hurried or allowed to degenerate into a brief nod.

Attitude in the dojo is important. Karateka should be quiet and only speak when spoken to by the senior. There should be no laughing, games or running around. When sitting on the floor, the knees must be drawn up and the legs crossed. Alternatively, the karateka can sit *seiza*, in a kneeling position, keeping the back straight with hands resting on the thighs. Under no circumstances should the karateka stretch out his legs or lie

Figure 3 Performing a standing bow or *rei*

on the dojo floor. The deportment of the student reflects his state of mind and indicates the standard of that particular dojo. Students model themselves upon their seniors and, if a bad example is set, they will follow.

At the commencement of the lesson, the class will be called to order by the senior (*sempai*) or by the teacher (*sensei*). The students form lines according to their rank and stand quietly waiting, with heels together and feet splayed. At the command 'Seiza', the class simultaneously adopts a kneeling posture. To do this, each student lowers himself down on his right knee, while keeping his back straight and arms to the side. He then lowers the left knee and sits back on his haunches, with head erect and back straight. The hands are placed palms down on the top of the thighs. The whole move is performed smoothly, deliberately and without haste.

The next command is 'Sensei ni rei' ('One bow to the teacher'). The class again moves as one, each sliding his hands to the ground in front of the knees and inclining the body forward (**figure 4**). The lowest position is maintained for a second, then the body returns to upright. The teacher returns the bow.

The third command is 'Otogai ni rei'. This is a bow to one's classmates and is performed by the students but not the teacher. In some dojo, there is an additional bow, which may be directed towards an object of veneration, such as a shrine or a memento from the founder of the ryu. When 'Kiritsu' is called, the class smoothly rises to its feet in the reverse order of kneeling.

Sometimes, while in seiza, the class will assume what is called *mokuso* (**figure 5**). This is a form of kneeling contemplation which involves closing the eyes and calming the mind. Breathing slows and becomes deep, with inhalation through the nose and exhalation through the mouth. Although it is at first impossible to keep the mind free of thought for more than a few instants of time, with perseverence a degree of success will be achieved. The result of meditation is always to refresh the mind, leaving it clear and alert.

Once the class is called to order, the students may no longer leave or enter the dojo as they please. Those arriving late will perform a standing bow in the doorway, then drop into seiza. After the two kneeling bows, they will remain kneeling, until beckoned in by the teacher. Karateka wishing to leave the dojo for any reason must first request permission of the teacher or, if he is busy, a class senior. At all times the student must be aware of the hierarchy which exists within the traditional dojo.

The lesser qualified student is known as the *kohei* and the senior as *sempai*. The junior grade always defers to the senior.

Figure 4 The kneeling bow

Figure 5 *Mokusu*, or kneeling contemplation

The grade system in karate

The Okinawan karate jutsu which gave rise to karatedo had no need for grades of competence since it was a fighting system in which you either excelled or failed. Master Chojun Miyagi made this point succinctly when he said that, if a student was good enough, he did not need a mark of competence such as a coloured belt; if he was not good enough, then he wouldn't get one anyway. Nevertheless, it was considered appropriate to institute a series of examinations, conducted at regular intervals during training, with the object of evaluating the student's competence and identifying it by means of a coloured belt.

At first there were only three colours of belt. The white belt was used to denote the novice; the green belt, the intermediate; and the brown belt, the advanced student. Later on, additional colours were added as the number of grading examinations increased. The coloured belt indicates what stage, or *kyu*, that the student has reached. A typical progression of belt colours is given here:

Novice	:	Red or white belt
8th kyu	:	White belt
7th kyu	:	Yellow belt
6th kyu	:	Orange belt
5th kyu	:	Green belt
4th kyu	:	Purple belt

3rd kyu
2nd kyu : Brown belt
1st kyu

1st dan : Black belt 1st level
2nd dan : Black belt 2nd level

There may be as few as six, or as many as ten, kyu grades in any ryu. In order to pass from one to another, the student takes a comprehensive examination based upon the techniques he has learned thus far. Those required for each grade are listed in the syllabus of the ryu. The average time which must elapse between gradings is three months, or forty-eight hours, whichever is the greater. In the case of the brown belts, ninety-six hours/six months must elapse between second and first kyu, first kyu and first dan.

The black belt is a mark of competence and is usually attained within five years of joining the club. There are stages within the black belt known as the *dan* grades and, as in the kyu grades, examinations are governed by the length of time a grade has been held. The following table is that of the World Union of Karatedo Organizations, the governing body for world karate.

2nd dan : 1st dan must be held for 2 years
3rd dan : 2nd dan must held for 3 years
4th dan : 3rd dan must be held for 4 years
5th dan : 4th dan must be held for 5 years
6th dan : 5th dan must be held for 6 years
7th dan : 6th dan must be held for 7 years
8th dan : 7th dan must be held for 8 years
9th dan : 8th dan must be held for 9 years
10th dan : 9th dan must be held for 10 years

Therefore a person who gained his first dan at the age of eighteen would, assuming he took and passed all of the intermediate grades, become a ninth dan at the age of sixty-two.

A tenth dan is the highest grade that can be awarded within a ryu. The founder, or *kancho*, may take this grade. Some founders consider that they are beyond grades in their ryu. Seventh and eighth dans are allowed to wear a belt that alternates red and white bands, while ninth and tenth dans wear all-red belts. Since the red belt is often used to denote the complete novice, the Master's return to red symbolizes the principle of karate-do, that he has 'forgotten' all technique and returned to the beginning.

With the grade held goes a specific title. Above sixth dan, the title of *shihan* (synonym = *hanshi*) is used. Between third and sixth dan, the title *sensei* applies. Below third dan, the correct title is *sempai*. If, however, a first or second dan operates his own dojo, then it is correct to call him sensei. The corps of black belts within a ryu are known as *yudansha*.

Advancements in grade up to and including the rank of third dan are taken by examination against the syllabus of the ryu. Above that level, they are conferred in recognition of diligent training.

Gradings are normally carried out by the sensei. He is empowered to examine students to within two or three grades below his own level. Therefore, a first dan may theoretically grade to third kyu brown belt, whereas a third dan may grade to first dan. In some ryu, only the Master is allowed to grade students. This has the advantage of ensuring the purity of the training and uniformity of standards.

The karateka carries a record of his training in the form of a licence book. Each time he advances a grade, the book is endorsed accordingly.

Training in karate
Once the class has completed its formal etiquette, training will begin with warm-up exercises. The purpose of these is to raise the temperature of the muscles, making them less prone to damage during sudden exertion. The basic form of training is performed in class lines. This is known as *kihon* and consists of individual basic techniques performed singly and with a pause in between. These techniques may consist of single punches, kicks, strikes or blocks. On the teacher's count, the class advances and performs the technique.

When space runs out, the whole class turns in unison, on the teacher's command 'Mawatte'. As they turn, they breathe out strongly in the form of a shout known as *kiai*. There is no adequate English translation of this word and, though the action seems obvious enough, the underlying principle is based on the concept of *ki*, the vital force. The kiai seeks to harmonize one's own vital force with that of the opponent and provides the impetus for physical action. The kiai is symbolic of the combination of spiritual resolve and physical action.

The kiai comes from the stomach and possesses a violence of sound that can shatter the opponent's composure. It is only genuine when there is total fusion of spirit with the body. Its rhythmic usage as an adjunct to basic training in some dojos shows a misunderstanding of its role within karate.

After practising basic techniques, the class moves on to combination moves (*renraku-waza*). These consist of several basic techniques linked together in a logical progression, with one move quickly following the next. Any combination of basic techniques can be used and, once the student becomes adept at running one technique on after another, he is encouraged to practise combinations where he selects the sequence. Practice of combination technique leads to fluidity of movement. The student capable of linking techniques in a quick and logical manner is never caught on the wrong foot and makes a formidable fighter.

Katas are used to teach techniques and principles. The nahate kata *sanchin*, for example, is the core of two Okinawan styles. Continued practice builds power and stability and conditions the body so it can better withstand the rigours of actual combat. The shurite kata *gankaku* teaches balance, speed and agility. Both start and finish on the same spot and consist of a series of combination techniques separated by pauses. The purpose of the techniques is explained by the training method known as kata *bunkai* ('analysis').

To the beginner, a kata is a confusing series of movements performed in different and at varying speeds. The rudiments of each take many months to learn. Yet once these have been mastered and the mind freed of concentration on mere technique, the kata becomes an expression of the meaning of karate. The mind is no longer preoccupied with remembering what comes next, but is able to meditate and increase awareness.

Yakusoku kimite is pre-arranged sparring practised between pairs of karateka. The attacker is called *tori* and the defender *uke*. Its object is to allow students safely to practise the principles of distance and timing in response to an attack. The attacker is given a specific technique to use, and the defender a specific counter. Therefore the parameters of the exercise are set in advance and the only variable is the relative abilities of the partners.

As experience develops, so the complexity and duration of the moves increase. Instead of a single attack, a combination can be used, so that, as each is successfully countered, another is launched. Repeated attack pre-arranged basic sparring is known as 'five-' or 'three-step sparring', depending upon the number of attacking moves made.

A more advanced form of pre-arranged sparring allows the karateka to adopt a more flexible approach. Although the attack and defence are still agreed beforehand, their execution is natural and takes place from a fighting stance. In *ji yu ippon kumite*, the attack is pre-selected and performed in a realistic manner. The defender, however, is free to choose his own counter. The teacher will assess the effectiveness of the defence chosen.

Free sparring (*ji yu kumite*) is normally practised only by the higher grades. Both attack and defence are unprogrammed, though certain techniques are prohibited because of the risk of injury associated with their use. Normally, substantial body contact is allowed between partners of equal weight, but strikes to the head are strictly controlled. In some cases the force of the attacks is limited by mutual agreement to touch contact. This allows the fighters more freedom and their techniques tend to be less guarded since the result of a mistake is less painfully pointed out.

The possibility of injury can be further lessened by wearing protective equipment. This takes the form of first mitts and shin, or shin and instep, protection. Fist mitts are foam pads made to fit over the knuckles. The fingers are left free, so they can be used for grabbing. Shin pads protect the vulnerable bones of the lower leg and instep pads extend forwards, down to the toes. Shin pads are either made up like pull-on elasticated stockings, or they are fastened with velcro. Men are advised to wear boxers' groin guards because, although low kicks are not allowed, accidents do happen.

Competition is a form of free sparring in which blows, strikes and kicks are delivered to scoring areas on the body, face and head with controlled force. The object is to score points for successful techniques. The success of any technique is assessed by the referee in consultation with an assistant, or 'mirror' referee. Competition in karate is well developed both nationally and internationally. Many clubs concentrate on free sparring and competition, though these represent only a small part of karate's syllabus.

Since much of karate's training is done with either no impact or with controlled impact there is little opportunity for full power strikes to be practised. The karateka who develops a perfect technique to the empty air may find it failing when used hard against a target. An impact can show shortcomings in technique in a way that no empty-air training can. A punch can bend sharply at the wrist because it has not been properly lined up; a front kick can damage the toes because they are not pulled back far enough. It follows that such is an essential part of effective karate practice. Normally, it is left to the student to make use of the facilities provided outside of the formal lesson.

The *makiwara* or punching post is now used far less

than it used to be. Its purpose is both to develop the force of blows and to harden the hands. Although the makiwara can be mounted against a wall, the traditional version is sunk into the soil of the garden to a depth of 1 metre and braced with rocks. It projects 1 metre and 40 centimetres above the ground and tapers in thickness from 12 centimetres at the submerged base to only 2 centimetres at the top. Its width is 12 centimetres throughout.

A pad of straw measuring 35 centimetres by 12 centimetres by 8 centimetres is made up and tied loosely together with thick string. The whole is then pounded with a mallet to compact it ready for use. It is bound to the face of the post and serves as the target for blows. When this is punched repeatedly, it causes the skin over the knuckles to redden. If training is carried on, the skin is soon rubbed off and the knuckles bleed. Since the post is well padded and sprung, bruising is not serious. If regular use is made of the makiwara, layers of hard skin form over the delicate knuckle joints, protecting them from damage, even during full power punches. Regular training with the makiwara will result in disfigurement of the hands and, for this reason, it is now little used. The makiwara is not suitable for practising kicks.

The punching pad and airbag are gaining ground in modern dojos. The former (**figure 6**) makes use of modern technology by assembling thick sheets of closed-

Figure 6 Using the impact bag

cell plastazote foam into a substantial pad capable of dissipating much of the force of a hard impact. The sheets are held together by enclosing them in a sewn canvas bag which has webbing straps stitched to the sides. In use, the pad is held against the chest by the straps. Full power techniques can be delivered into it, with only the shock of the blow being transmitted to the holder.

Because the pad is not hard, damage to the knuckles is slight, though reddening can occur after prolonged training. If the pad is being used as a target for very strong techniques, then, instead of holding it against the chest, the partner can use the webbing straps to hold it against the shoulder and fully bent arm. Once the attacker becomes used to hitting the stationary pad, his partner can move it forwards and back, thus giving him the chance to attack a moving target. A pocket in the back allows the pad to be held by a single hand if desired. The pad can vary in size and some are made large, enabling them to be used for kicks. As well as this, the pad can be used to painlessly train blocking techniques by swinging it on its webbing straps into the defender.

The airbag is a light, inflatable pad with loops through which an arm can be inserted. It is very easy to use and causes little damage to the knuckles even when used hard over long periods. Light punchbags are also good training aids for impact training.

CHAPTER 4: THE STANCES OF KARATE

The purpose of stances
The stances of karate are platforms from which techniques may be effectively used. They represent responses to situations, allowing the karateka to make the right move in the right direction, in the right way. A stance may be maintained or changed as the situation alters. The wise usage of stance ensures that the karateka will never be caught off guard.

The stance is used to guard against an attack, and subsequently to evade and counter it. During combat, distances may close or open and the karateka must therefore learn how to maintain, by judicious use of stance, the optimal distance between himself and his opponent (*ma-ai*). Therefore he must be capable of moving equally well in all directions, maintaining an effective guard as he does so. Because no combat is fixed in distance or direction, stances must not be rigidly held. The speed with which they are formed and changed is a vital element in the success of any combat.

Different stances have different applications. Some, like *sanchin*, develop strength and condition the body. Others, like *neko-ashi*, are fighting stances which favour the usage of some techniques over others. Between them are steps and half steps, all of which must be performed correctly and without .hesitation to aid transfer of weight and speed of body movement. Each stance is a combination of three components – length, width and height. Length confers fore and aft stability and allows the use of penetrating techniques that drive into the opponent. The longer the stance, the stronger this component. When pushing a motor car, a long stance concentrates power forwards. A wide stance gives lateral stability, preventing balance from being upset by a sideways pull or push.

A low stance gives a correspondingly low centre of gravity and greater power in slower-acting techniques such as a push or shove. A high stance gives less support yet allows greater mobility and speed of movement. It does not weaken high-energy impact techniques where body movement is needed to absorb recoil.

Attention stance
Attention stance (**figure 7**) is known by various Japanese names, the most common of which are *musubi-dachi*

Figure 7 Attention stance with heels together and hands opened

and *heisoku-dachi*. It is the stance from which the standing bow (*ritsu rei*) is performed. To assume it, the back is straightened and the head held high. The chin is pulled in and the gaze directed forwards. The heels are brought together and the feet point outwards at a 45-degree angle. The hands hang naturally to the sides, with palms resting lightly against the sides of the thighs. As a slight variation on this stance, some ryu advocate closing the fists and holding the arms straight and slightly away from the body. The muscles of the stomach are relaxed and weight concentrated in the lower part of the body.

Attention stance has no fighting significance. It is a relaxed but prepared stance to be adopted when the opponent is at a good distance.

Ready stance

On the command 'Yoi', the ready stance (**figure 8**) is assumed from attention stance. The feet are separated and turn only slightly outwards, first the left moving to the side – then the right. The outside edges of the feet finish up approximately shoulder-width apart. The arms move away from the thighs and the fists clench. The body is upright, with the head held high and chin pulled in. Breathing is measured and every effort is made to relax the muscles in preparation for rapid movement.

This stance is to be used when the opponent has closed distance but is still outside effective attacking range. To reduce the risk of being caught unawares by a sudden attack, the stance can be turned 45 degrees to the opponent. By this means, a narrower target is presented and the body's vulnerable areas slightly withdrawn.

Some styles move firmly into ready stance, exhaling strongly, distending the stomach and tightening the fists. This has the effect of concentrating awareness and strengthening resolve.

Ready stance is known as *hachiji-dachi*.

Natural stance

Natural stance is also called *shizentai*. It is derived from ready stance by sliding the left or right foot a half pace forwards and slightly inwards. The body remains erect with head held high, arms relaxed and fists clenched as in ready stance. It is important to keep all the weight over the rear foot, so the front is just resting lightly. From this position, a sudden forward movement – either direct or inclined – can be made.

If the left foot leads, the stance is called *hidari-shizentai*; if the right leads, *migi-shizentai*. Shizentai may be used when the opponent has closed to near effective range.

Figure 8 Ready stance with heels apart and fists clenched

Cat stance

Cat stance (**figure 9**), or *nekoashi-dachi*, follows on from natural stance. The front foot moves a little further out from the body and into line with the rear foot. The rear leg bends at the knee, concentrating almost the entire body weight down upon it. The body is lowered but remains perfectly upright above the supporting leg, with the head erect. The front leg also bends at the knee, though less so than the rear. The front heel lifts off the floor, leaving the ball of the foot lightly touching. The hips face directly forwards.

The weight distribution can be tested by lifting the front foot. If there is a tendency to fall forwards, not enough weight has been concentrated over the rear foot. This can be remedied by straightening the back and bringing the rear hip squarely above the back leg.

From this stance, the front leg can be quickly used as a snapping kick since it is easily moved without loss of posture.

Back stance

Back stance (**figure 10**) is a lengthened form of cat stance. Its Japanese name is *kokutsu-dachi*. It differs from cat stance in its weight distribution, with the rear leg now carrying between 70 and 75 percent body weight, and the front, 25 to 30 percent. The body remains upright but, because of the increased length of stance, the hips are now inclined 45 degrees forward facing, instead of square on. In some ryu, the body moves slightly off the rear leg. This is responsible for the change in weight distribution. The heel of the rear foot remains in line with the forward-facing front foot.

The front foot may either rest flat on the floor or the heel may be raised, as in cat stance. The rear foot is either turned out 90 degrees to the front foot, or turned 45 degrees towards it. The angle of the rear foot determines the degree to which the body is turned. A full 90 degrees angle between the feet leaves the body sideways facing.

The back stance is very good for blocking. The face and body are kept back out of harm's way and the bent back leg can function as a spring, driving the body forwards into the attack.

Straddle stance

Straddle stance (**figure 11**) is also known as 'horseriding stance'. It can be assumed from back stance by simply moving the body midway between the feet and turning it in the direction of the open thighs. The feet rotate so they are either equally pointing outwards or equally pointing slightly inwards. The back must be kept straight and the bottom tucked in. The shoulders are

Figure 9 Cat stance has all the weight on the near leg

Figure 10 Back stance

pulled back and the head is held erect. The distribution of weight is 50 per cent on each leg.

It is important to ensure that the knees are above the insteps. There is a tendency to have the feet too wide apart with the result that a plumb line hung from the inside of the knees would touch the floor inside the feet. This makes for a weak stance and must be avoided. The more correct the stance, the more vertical the lower legs will be. The correct width of the stance will vary according to the ryu but, generally, twice shoulder width is correct.

If the feet are parallel or slightly diverging, the stance is called *shiko-dachi*. It is encountered not only in karate but also in sumo wrestling. If the feet are converging, the whole character of the stance changes. The feet grip the ground along their outer edges and the hips are forced forwards and up. The knees rotate outwards, creating a twisting sensation in the lower legs. This is an immensely strong but fatiguing stance called *kiba-dachi*.

Figure 11 Straddle or 'horseriding' stance.

Immovable stance

This can be formed from straddle stance by rotating the front foot forwards and bending the front knee. The rear knee is forced outwards and the body held upright and twisted to the front. The feet are more or less parallel and the hips are 45 degrees forward facing. The stance is very strong and versatile and allows blocking, kicking and punching techniques to be used with equal favour. It is also a fluid stance and allows rapid movement.

Immovable stance is non-traditional and was created in 1934 by the Shotokan school. It reflected a first attempt to create a stance lower and more regular than the original high stances taught by Gichin Funakoshi. It is not a common stance in modern karate but occurs extensively in the Shotokai. Its Japanese name is *fudo-dachi*.

Semi-forward Stance

This stance, called *moroashi-dachi*, (**figure 12**) is midway between immovable stance and the fully developed forward stance. From 45 degrees forward facing, the hips and shoulders turn square onto the front. The front foot moves outward and the rear foot swivels so it is parallel. Both knees are well bent.

This is very much an action stance with great potential energy. The straightening of the rear leg drives the body forwards behind a high energy punch, or a deflection of a descending blow close to source. It is a technique delivery stance in its own right and is ideal for unspecialized close range work.

Figure 12 Semi-forward stance

Forward Stance

Forward stance, or *zenkutsu-dachi*, (**figure 13**) is a further development of the Shotokan school and the logical next stage in the lowering of immovable stance, or the extending of semi-forward stance. The weight remains equally distributed between the front and back legs and the hips are pulled around until they are forward facing. The front foot points directly forwards and the rear one is as parallel to it as possible. Care must be taken not to bend the rear knee and the leg remains locked straight.

The front knee is well bent and lies directly above the instep. The back is upright, or leaning slightly forward in line with the sweep of the back leg to give a greater forward thrust. Care should be taken when leaning into the stance, to avoid thrusting the face forwards. The length of forward stance varies between the ryu, with Shotokan having a characteristically deep stance and Wado ryu being much higher. Shito ryu lies midway between the two. The width of the stance is fairly common and can be checked by bending the rear knee down to the ground and measuring the width between it and the heel of the leading foot. The correct distance is the width of two fists held thumb to thumb.

Figure 13 *Zentkutsu-dachi*, or forward stance. Hips are forward facing

The stability of forward stance can be tested with the aid of a partner. Tori stands in left stance and extends his left fist, locking the elbow. Uke then advances to the leading fist until it comes to press against his breast bone. Pressure is then exerted against it. If tori's front foot begins to rise from the ground, or his upper body is forced back, he is not leaning forward enough.

Reverse Punch Stance

Reverse punch stance (**figure 14**) is very similar to forward stance and developed from it. The front foot is brought slightly backwards and outwards, and rotates to point inwards. Weight is settled on the outside edge of the foot. The hips are twisted fully square on and the rear foot rotates so it faces forwards, making the feet parallel, or slightly converging. In classic reverse punch stance, the rear leg is locked straight.

Half Moon Stance

Half moon stance (*hangetsu-dachi* or *seishan-dachi*) is an unusual stance. It is very traditional and is performed in two distinct ways. The feet are parallel or slightly converging and the knees are equally bent. Weight distribution is equal between the two legs. The stance is aligned 45 degrees forward facing. The Shotokan school has the knees pressing inwards, with the back straight. The Okinawan schools force the knees outwards and push the hips up and forwards so the legs

Figure 14 Reverse punch stance. The punching hip is forward

are in tension. Their version looks like a foreshortened and inclined kibadachi. Held in this manner, the stance is very strong and stable under attack.

Hourglass Stance

This is the sanchin stance beloved of the nahate school (**figure 15**). It is found most frequently in Goju ryu and Uechi ryu and is there used as the basis for the whole style. It is tremendously rigid and resistant to all attempts at unbalancing.

To adopt it, the half moon stance is shortened until the toes of the rear foot are in line with the heel of the front foot. The feet are twisted asymmetrically, with the front twisted 45 degrees inwards, the rear turned until its toes are facing the front foot. The knees are forced out and the hips driven forwards. Weight distribution remains equal over both legs. The stance is upright and quite short but possesses a stability out of all proportion to its length. Owing to the combination of length and width, the stance is firm in all directions. The Shotokan version has the knees forced inwards.

Sanchin is a tension stance which develops powerful leg and stomach muscles.

Fighting Stance

During sparring, many techniques will be used and stances must change to meet the new requirements. When closing range in preparation to exchange techniques, fighting stance (*ju-dachi*) (**figure 16**) is adopted. The height of this stance will vary according to individual preference but it should neither be so long as to slow down movement nor so high as to make the user likely to be swept off his feet in the fury of an attack. Weight distribution is equal and both knees are bent, giving a springy, unspecialized stance that can move quickly in all directions.

The feet are turned slightly inwards, so the groin is closed and the body turned 45 degrees onto the opponent. This narrows the width of body target the opponent can see and allows the rear hand a good distance in which to accelerate a telling punch. The stance includes a lateral element and this should neither be so wide as to open the groin to attack nor too narrow, leading to weak balance.

Moving from Stance to Stance

When moving from one stance to another, the height should remain constant, with no bobbing up and down. During the step, the body is not stable and cannot mount a strong defence. Therefore it must be made quickly. The form the step takes will depend entirely upon the stances used.

Figure 15 Hourglass stance.

Figure 16 Fighting stance

When stepping from forward stance to forward stance, the front knee is kept well bent and the rear foot drawn up, alongside and past. The rear foot skims lightly over the floor and, when it reaches its final position, sets down gently on the ball of the foot first, then on the heel as weight settles (**figures 17, 18, 19**). The rear foot must travel forwards in a straight line and a tendency to bring it up into the mid-line avoided since this narrows the stance and impairs balance. Fighting stance is advanced in a similar way.

The technique is slightly different for reverse punch. In this case, the front foot first rotates outwards, then the rear foot slides forwards and inwards until it comes alongside. It then continues travelling forwards and outwards to its final position. The path of the rear foot is therefore a very shallow 'U' shape (**figures 20, 21, 22**). This semicircular step is encountered a great deal in stances where the hips are to be used to lend power to a blow. Some schools step directly forwards, claiming this gives extra speed to the advance. Both half moon and hourglass stances use the semi-circular step when advancing.

The natural, cat and back stances all advance by setting the weight firmly on the front foot and stepping through with the rear leg. It is important here to ensure that the newly positioned front foot settles not only in front of, but also in line with, the other.

Straddle stance advances by means of the transient scissors stance. Body weight shifts forwards over the leading leg and the rear comes up to and crosses by it. The foot can either pass to the front or behind the supporting leg and weight is put on it. The supporting leg then slides forwards and resumes the leading position (**figures 23, 24, 25, overleaf**). This move is quite fluid but, during it, the back must be kept straight and not allowed to tilt as weight is transferred.

The Turn

It is very important to turn quickly so as to meet a threat coming from a new direction. Regardless of the starting stance, the most important thing to do first is to glance over the shoulder, to check that no attack is imminent from that direction.

Different ryu turn in different ways, some stressing hip movement, others ignoring it. The mechanism of the turn will depend upon the stance employed but falls into two basic types. If the stance has unequal weight distribution, such as natural, cat or back stance, the first move involves sliding the front foot sideways a short distance, then settling it down and transferring weight onto it by moving the body forwards.

Weight is transferred through the ball of the foot and

Figure 17 About to advance from forward stance to forward stance

Figure 18 When stepping from forward stance to forward stance, let the rear foot skim lightly over the floor

Figure 19 Advance to forward stance completed

Figure 20 About to advance from reverse punch

Figure 21 Advancing from reverse punch: hips kept back

Figure 22 Completion of the semi-circular step and hip driving forwards

the hips rotate in the direction the step was made. As weight comes off the original supporting leg, it becomes free to pivot, forming the front foot of the new stance. The turn is not quite as sequential as it reads and the action of settling the weight occurs concurrently with the hip-twist and pivoting of the front leg, giving a rapid movement.

In most stances where there is equal weight distribution, no transfer of weight is needed and the body remains fixed relative to the legs, merely rotating to face in the new direction. In the case of forward, semi-forward, fighting (**figure 26**) or immovable stances, the first action is to step across with the rear leg, sliding it along on the ball of the foot. If a line is drawn straight back from the heel of the front foot, the sliding rear foot will move an equidistance from one side of it to the other. When making this step, it is important not to bring the foot forwards. If this happens, the new stance will be foreshortened.

It is also important to step across the imaginary line from the front heel, otherwise the new stance will have no lateral stability and balance will be lost (**figure 27**).

During the turn, both legs are well bent and the height of the stance maintained. There is a tendency to bob up and down and this must be avoided. Once the rear foot is correctly positioned, the hips rotate in the direction taken by that foot. The upper body remains forward facing as the hips begin to turn and this creates a torsional stress in the back muscles. As the hips continue to turn, the upper body is released and twists sharply, ending up facing in the reverse direction. As the rotation concludes, weight is returned to the new front foot (**figure 28**).

Straddle stance involves quite a different and much simpler turning mechanism. The person in straddle stance is normally side-on to the opponent. Were he front facing, his groin would be wide open to *kin-geri* (groin kick). To turn, therefore, all the karateka needs to do is suddenly to twist the upper body through a right angle so that it finishes facing the other way.

A mirror is useful when practising stance changes and turns. The student should practise moving quickly from one stance into the next, using fast, concise movements that can twist the body out of danger. The change in stance to evade an attack is known as *tai-sabaki* or body movement.

Figure 23 Advancing straddle stance by means of the transient scissors stance

Figure 24 Advancing straddle stance: the rear foot passing to the front of the supporting leg

Figure 25 Advancing straddle stance: the supporting leg has slid forward

Figure 26 The turn: about to step across with the rear leg

Figure 27 The turn: stepping across the imaginary line from the front heel

Figure 28 The turn completed: the hips turn in the new direction

CHAPTER 5: THE WEAPONS OF KARATE

Karate is a fighting system which depends upon high-impact blows, kicks and strikes. The weapons of karate are any parts of the body with sufficient mass and which can be accelerated enough to develop significant kinetic energy. In addition, they must be relatively insensitive to pain yet hard enough to cause the opponent injury.

The weapons of the untrained body are often delicate and as likely to cause injury to the user as they are to the victim. Therefore the serious karateka will condition those weapons until they are capable of withstanding impact. The knuckles can be conditioned by means of makiwara. The fingers are strengthened by plunging them into tubs of sawdust, and grip is improved by using a spring frame or the traditional but effective *kame*.

The Weapons of the Hand

Front fist
The front fist (**figure 29**) is the most commonly used weapon in karate. It is difficult to form properly and, in the unconditioned hand, the skin over the knuckles is thin, leading to laceration and bruising in use. The unconditioned fist should only be used against soft targets, avoiding contact with bone and teeth.

To form a front fist, the fingers are folded into the palm. The fold is fairly tight and brings the fingertips against the fleshy pad which runs along the base of the fingers. The fist is locked by folding the thumb across the middle of the index finger. The thumb should not project forwards, where it can catch in loose clothing and dislocate. Neither should it be folded inside the fist.

A profile of the fist reveals a right angle between the back of the hand and the folded fingers. This angle is important if the finger joints are not to connect painfully with the target. The fist should be repeatedly formed until it has the correct angle. Protruding finger joints can be forced back by making a fist and leaning on it against the top of a table.

The effort of holding a fist tightly closed fatigues the muscles of the lower arm and slows down punch delivery. It is therefore a good idea to hold the fist correctly but loosely, and close it suddenly and forcefully the instant before impact.

Figure 29 Front fist

The angle the fist makes with the target is important and, when punching upwards, the first parts to impact are the joints of the fingers. For this reason, the fist is rotated thumb uppermost. The lower the target, the more the fist rotates palm down on impact. This rotation is accomplished by the muscles of the lower arm. The smaller knuckles describe an arc around those of the index and middle finger.

On impact, these two knuckles are furthest forward and their supporting metacarpals must be in a straight line with the radius and ulnar bones of the lower arm. If this is not correctly configured, the wrist will flex and perhaps break on impact. Front fist must be tested against a makiwara or impact pad since punching only against the air will not show up faults of this nature.

The elbow of the punching arm must lock on impact, so no energy is wasted by the arm flexing. The impact must be focused over the smallest possible area if it is to have the greatest effect. This is best explained by an analogy. Consider the effect of being pushed in the chest by someone using the flat of their hands and then by someone holding a sharpened pencil. The pencil will cause greater pain because it channels its force over a much smaller area. This principle is used in karate and the front fist impacts only on the two largest knuckles.

The front fist is known in Japanese as *seiken*.

Back fist
Back fist is delivered with a whip-lash action that unrolls the arm into the target. The front fist configuration is used but impact is made with the back of the knuckles

Figure 30 Horizontal back fist　　Figure 31 The arm unrolls into the target

of the index and middle fingers. The wrist must be kept relaxed and able to snap out when the driving arm is abruptly stopped.

Back fist can be used as a horizontal or vertical strike. The former is usually aimed at the side of the face, the latter to the bridge of the nose. When attacking the side of the face, the hips rotate in the opposite direction to the strike and weight is transferred onto the front foot. The elbow of the striking arm is bent and raised until it points to the target (**figure 30**). The lower arm is then released and the fist travels up and outwards in an arc (**figure 31**). Back fist has a long range and is extremely fast and difficult to block.

To deliver back fist vertically the forearm is held upright and use is made of forward body movement such as that following a front kick. Distance is quickly closed and the fist driven out and snapped back, like cracking a whip. Used in this way, the technique has a short range.

Back fist is known as *uraken*.

One-knuckle fist
One-knuckle fist is an excellent way of focusing power into the target. It is not as strong as a front fist and is generally used to attack the opponent's weak points (**figure 32**). There are two forms of one-knuckle punch, each originating from a separate source. The more common form is derived from the Okinawan school of nahate and uses the middle finger to deliver impact. This is called *nakadaka-ipponken*. A normal front fist configuration is used but the middle finger is pushed out so its middle joint protrudes. It is locked out by the 'V' caused through closing the index and fourth fingers together with pressure from the thumb.

Figure 32 One-knuckle fist

Figure 33 Beginning the hammer fist

The second form, called *ipponken*, is derived from Shaolin wushu. This uses the middle knuckle of the index finger which is locked out by the thumb. A little practice locks the knuckle out very firmly and, with conditioning, this technique can become one of the best weapons in the karateka's armoury. It is ideal for use against the ribs, solar plexus and temple.

Hammer fist
Hammer fist uses a front fist configuration but, here the impact area is the ridge of muscle between the little finger and the wrist. This is well cushioned but care must be taken not to catch the bones of the wrist or the base of the little finger.

Figure 34 The impact of hammer fist

Figure 35 Semi-open fist, or *hiraken*

The fist is raised above the head and brought crashing down on the target. Its force is increased by bending the knees on impact. This adds the momentum of the body to the force of the swing. At the moment of impact, all the muscles of the body become momentarily rigid, concentrating energy into the strike.

Hammer fist is particularly effective against the head, or when used with a backwards swing into the opponent's groin.

The Japanese name for hammer fist is *tettsui*.

Semi-open fist
Semi-open fist, or *hiraken*, is an unusual weapon used against the ribs, diaphragm and angle of the jaw (**figure 35**). It is formed from front fist by opening the fingers away from the palm, but keeping the fingertips pressed against the pad of flesh at their base. The thumb presses against the tip of the index finger and the impact area is the middle joints of the fingers.

The semi-open fist is normally delivered without twisting the fist. On impact, the muscles of the lower arm abruptly tighten. The strike is not a high energy one but is useful as a diversion which creates an opening for a more powerful follow-up.

The experienced karateka uses strikes like semi-open fist to attack what are called the vital points. These are areas of the body where an impact produces an effect out of all proportion to the power used. Skilful use of vital points can paralyse, stun, or even kill.

Palm heel
Palm heel, or *taisho*, is an excellent weapon to use

Figure 36 Palm heel, or *taisho*

Figure 37 Spear head, or *nukite*

because it cuts out the troublesome wrist joint and delivers its impact over the padded heel of the hand. The technique is formed by bending back the wrist of semi-open fist.

The Shaolin wushu schools make great use of palm heel but usually extend the fingers. On delivery, the fingers flex back and the base of the palm is driven into the target. Palm heel is ideal for attacking body targets and may be used with safety against the temple or jaw (**figure 36**).

Spear hand
Spear hand, or *nukite*, uses a fully open hand to deliver strikes with the fingertips. The fingers are extended and the thumb folded across the palm. At the moment of impact, the fingers stiffen. The average person cannot use spear hand with any force simply because the fingers flex back and dislocation easily occurs. Trained karateka, however, are able to slightly withdraw the middle finger so it comes into line with the tips of those on either side.

Conditioning produces a dangerous weapon, capable of delivering a great deal of force over a very small area. The fully conditioned fingertips can be thrust through an inch or two of wooden board with no problem whatsoever.

Spear hand was a favourite technique of the Okinawan to-de Master.

A single finger spear thrust can be used against the eye or throat (**figure 37**). The index finger is extended but the other fingers fold back against the top of the palm. This technique is known as *ippon nukite*. There is also a double finger variation known as *nihon nukite*. This uses the extended and separated index and middle fingers to attack both eyes simultaneously.

Figure 38 Knife hand

Knife hand

Knife hand, or *shuto*, is rather unjustifiably taken as the trademark of karate. It is often referred to as 'the karate chop', even when used by other martial arts. Knife hand can be used either as a block or as a weapon, but in this section only the latter usage will be considered.

To form knife hand, the hand is opened out fully and the thumb folded and clamped to the palm. The hand cups slightly and is held absolutely rigid at the moment of impact (**figure 38**). Like hammer fist, the impact area is that pad of flesh which runs along the edge of the hand between the little finger and the bones of the wrist.

Knife hand can be used in a variety of ways, depending upon the target. To attack the neck, the karateka stands with left foot forward in a fighting stance and draws back the right hand, palm uppermost. For maximum power, the arm must be drawn well back and bent at the elbow. The other extends forward and is withdrawn simultaneously with the strike.

The hips swing to the left and, a moment later, the upper body follows. The hand is kept palm upwards as it swings across and into the side of the opponent's neck. As it is about to contact, the wrist suddenly twists around and cuts into the neck with a cupping action.

Knife hand can also be used the reverse way. The karateka stands in right fighting stance and brings his right arm back over the left shoulder, cupping the ear. The hips swing around and, a moment later, the shoulders follow. Just before impact, the knife hand suddenly twists palm down. The final twisting action gains extra power for the technique.

Figure 39 Ridge hand

Knife hand can also be used as a descending strike against the collarbone. The karateka stands in left fighting stance and raises his right hand high and to the rear, with the palm facing away. The hips turn into the target and the shoulders follow behind. The hand travels in a downwards arc and the little finger turns down on impact. Flexing the knees at the same time gives a bonus in power.

Ridge hand
Ridge hand, or *haito*, uses the same configuration as knife hand but impacts on the index finger side (**figure 39**). The thumb must be pressed in as far as it will go, to avoid damage to the joint. An alternative form closes the fist but leaves the thumb joint projecting outwards. The tip of the thumb braces against the base of the index finger. This is very effective for lower powered strikes to weak areas such as the temple or the angle of the jaw. A circular motion combined with body evasion is used to deliver the technique.

Claw hand
Claw hand is a low-energy strike delivered to the face, or anywhere there is loose flesh which may be grasped. The hand position resembles palm heel except that the fingers are curled like hooks.

The technique is driven straight out like palm heel but, upon contact, the fingers curl in and grasp. It is particularly effective against the face (**figure 40**, overleaf). It is also very effective when used as an underhand snatch at the groin.

Figure 40 Claw hand

To improve claw hand, grip strengthening exercises should be practised.

The wrist
The back of the wrist, or *koken,* is a useful if little-used weapon. It can be employed after a hooking block pulls the opponent's front guard down. Body weight is transferred forwards and the bent wrist slammed into the nose, using a last-minute flexion to increase power.

The elbow
The elbow is a very powerful weapon but can only be used when close to the opponent. In use, the striking elbow is pulled back and the fist rotated thumb upwards, to protect the funny bone. Impact is always made with the point of the elbow and not with the forearm. In this way, force is concentrated over the smallest possible area. There are five ways of using elbow strike.

The first can be practised from a left fighting stance. The right hip twists forwards and the right shoulder follows. The striking elbow is fully bent and the fist carried close to the chest. The elbow moves in an arc, striking the side of the opponent's jaw with a glancing impact.

The second is delivered from the same stance but uses a vertical strike which travels upwards and impacts under the chin like a short-range uppercut.

The third form is used when the karateka is sideways on to his opponent. If his right side is closest, then the right arm moves across the chest and the left arm extends forward beneath it, with the hand opened. The left arm is strongly pulled back and, at the same time, the right elbow is driven into the attacker's ribs or face. To increase the impact, body weight should be transferred in the direction of the strike and the left hand pulled into a fist.

The fourth is used against an opponent standing to the rear. The karateka first looks over his shoulder to gauge the range and then steps back. The length of this step is critical; too much and he will body crash into his opponent, too little and the elbow will not reach. As the step is completed, body weight is quickly transferred backwards over it. The hips swivel in the direction of the strike.

If the right foot has been used to step back, then the right hand reaches forwards, fingers extended. As weight settles on the back foot and the hips twist into the opponent, the extended hand is strongly pulled back and, at the moment of impact, closes into a fist.

This whole sequence of moves produces an extremely powerful technique which is targeted onto the opponent's solar plexus or breastbone (**figure 41**).

If the opponent has first been doubled up by a knee into his stomach, then a descending elbow, the fifth method, can be used. The striking arm reaches high into the air, with fingers uncurled, and is brought quickly down with the hand closing into a fist on impact. To use this method successfully the user must be standing

Figure 41 Elbow strike to the opponent's solar plexus

Figure 42 Front kick, showing the instep at the moment of delivery

Figure 43 The instep used as a weapon for attacking the groin

Figure 44 The heel swings high above the head in an axe kick

Figure 45 The heel brought down on the target in an axe kick

very close to the victim and must flex his knees on impact, so the momentum of the body is added to the force of the strike.

The main impact energy of elbow strikes comes from the body and upper arms. There are no weak joints to flex upon impact and, as a result, the technique can be very effective.

The Japanese term for the elbow is *hiza*.

The Techniques of the Foot

The ball of the foot

The ball of the foot is an excellent weapon, combining padding with a narrow impact area that concentrates force efficiently. The toes must be pulled back out of the way if they are to escape injury. In front kick, the instep is in line with the shin at the moment of delivery (**figure 42**), whereas in roundhouse kick the foot is at right angles to it.

The beginner usually experiences difficulty with the front kick. Either the toes are not pulled back far enough and crash into the target with painful results or the foot is pulled upwards and impact made with the sole. The latter is less painful but it is also ineffective. To practise foot position for front kick, the karateka lifts his heel as far off the ground as possible, while keeping the ball of the foot pressed firmly down.

The ball of the foot is called *koshi* in Japanese.

The instep

The instep (*heisoku*) is an ideal weapon for attacking the groin (**figure 43**) and thighs. It is also very effective when used against the side of the jaw. The foot is fully extended and the toes curled down. Every effort must be made to keep the instep in line with the shin. Impact is made with the part of the instep nearest to the ankle; any further out can cause the ankle or toes to bend painfully. Care must also be taken accurately to target the technique because a badly bruised foot can result when the instep collides into the opponent's knee or elbow.

The heel

The heel (*kakato*), like the ball of the foot, can be used in several ways. In axe kick, the leg is swung high above the head (**figure 44**) and the heel brought down onto the target using the combined effects of leg weight and acceleration due to gravity (**figure 45**). The ball of the foot is pulled back out of the way.

In side kick, the foot is held at right angles to the shin, with the sole parallel to the floor (**figure 46**). The big toe is lifted and the other toes turned downwards. This is a difficult posture and requires much practice. Alternatively, all the toes can be lifted – it does not matter as long as the heel is projecting and makes first contact with the target.

Although the heel makes first contact in a side kick, the outside edge of the foot (*sokuto*) also serves as a secondary impact weapon, concentrating force along a narrow strip.

Back kick uses the same foot configuration as axe

Figure 46 Side kick: the foot is held at right angles to the shin

Figure 47 Using the inside edge of the foot to knock the opponent's guard to one side

kick. The ball of the foot is pulled back and the heel projects furthest. The ball of the foot points as near vertically downwards as possible.

The inside edge of the foot
The inside edge of the foot is useful for scooping up the opponent's foot or knocking his guard to one side in preparation for an attack (**figure 47**).

Foot sweep (*ashi barai*) sweeps the outer edge of the foot over the ground and into the back of the opponent's weight-bearing leg. Power is generated by the hips and the body leans back from possible counter-attack. A successful foot sweep can drop the opponent onto his back, leaving him vulnerable.

Crescent kick (*mikazuki geri*) also uses the inner edge of the foot but holds it vertically instead of parallel with the floor.

The knee
The knee is an excellent close-range weapon. It can be used against the opponent's groin and, if his head is pulled down, against the chest or face (**figure 48**). During delivery, the back arches and the toes point towards the ground. Care must be taken to strike with the point of the knee rather than with the muscles of the thigh. When using the knee as a weapon, extra power can be injected by raising the body up onto the ball of the supporting foot. This adds momentum to the force of the blow.

The Japanese term for the knee is *hiza*.

Effective Targets

The weapons described above are of use only if they make hard enough contact with the effective targets on the opponent's head and body. In Japanese, these targets are known as *kyusho*.

The head is a vulnerable target and any hard blow to it will cause brain damage. The extent of damage and duration of symptoms will vary according to the force used. At certain points the skull is less thick and a blow there can have serious repercussions. The temple (*komekami*) is one such weak point and a one-knuckle punch there may cause unconsciousness or even coma.

The eyes are extremely vulnerable to open-handed attacks. Even the lightest touch will evoke floods of tears and blur vision. More powerful strikes can damage the eyeball, causing haemorrhage and blindness.

The ears may be damaged by clapping a cupped hand over them. This compresses the air in the outer ear and ruptures the eardrum.

The nose is well equipped with sensory nerves and a

Figure 48 Pulling the head down enables the knee to be used as a weapon for attacking the chest

hard blow can cause copious bleeding and floods of tears. The lips are easily cut when caught between a punch and the teeth. The teeth can cause severe cuts to the fist and, because of the bacteria present in the mouth, sepsis can result.

If the chin (*kakon*) is caught with a blow, the head is jarred and unconsciousness can result. A blow to the side of the jaw is more likely to produce a knock out because of the twisting motion it causes.

The neck carries the windpipe, spinal column, several major blood vessels and nerves. A hard blow there can break the neck vertebrae, causing death. It can also rupture the voice box which is protected only by cartilage. Lower down, a hard blow can rupture the windpipe with possibly fatal results.

The collarbones (*shofu*) lie close to the surface and can be broken with knife hand strike. This produces severe pain and stops the opponent from using his arms. The solar plexus (*suigetsu*) consists of a bundle of nerve fibres. A hard blow there causes contraction of the diaphragm and chest muscles, resulting in difficult breathing.

A sharp blow to the breastbone can produce a reflexive spasm of the psoas muscles. These cause the arms and legs to fly forwards, sending the victim backwards and off balance. A blow which compresses the chest can interrupt heart rhythm and cause death.

The spleen is a reservoir of blood and, when ruptured, leads to shock and death if untreated. The spleen can be damaged by a hard kick which lands beneath the ribs on the left side of the stomach. A hard kick on the right side can damage the liver and produce jaundice.

The spine can be damaged by a hard kick and resultant whip-lash injuries to the neck will exacerbate the situation. The kidneys can also be damaged by a kick to the back, releasing blood into the urine.

Even a light kick to the groin produces the most severe pain, causing the sufferer difficulty in breathing. This is because injury to the cremaster muscle sends waves of sympathetic contraction through the muscles of the stomach and chest. Kicks to the inside or outside of the thighs can numb the leg. The kneecap and instep are vulnerable to stamping kicks.

CHAPTER 6: THE BLOCKS OF KARATE

A block is a movement of the body or its limbs which interrupts an attacking technique, preventing it from landing on the target it was aimed for. The attack can be made to miss, in which case it is said to be evaded, or it can be actually halted by means of a block. A combination of evasion and block will provide the safest counter to any attack.

There are two types of block — one which meets a technique's strength and defeats it and one which accepts an attack and redirects it harmlessly. The first type is effective when used by strongly built karateka. Chojun Miyagi used only blocking techniques when he sparred with students but these were so powerful that they caused injury to the attacker's limbs. For those less strong, deflection blocks provide an excellent means of dealing with even the most powerful attacker.

A deflection block does not meet the full force of an attack head on but seeks rather to harmonize with it by taking a path with it either parallel to and in the same direction, or obliquely intersecting. The attack is gently channelled a different way and its own force used to defeat it. The deflection block is greatly assisted by body movement which puts it in the correct position and angle.

Body movement alone can cause a technique to miss through simple evasion. All attacks are aimed at a specific target and movement of that target may well cause them to miss. The object is to cause the attacker's techniques to miss while remaining in a position where an effective counter can be used. Therefore, when making a body evasion, only the minimum distance compatible with safety should be used.

The direction in which the attack is coming will provide a clue as to which way to move. An incoming front kick can be avoided by stepping back but, as soon as it lands, the attacker can resume attacking unhindered and the moment of truth is only delayed. It is far better to step to the side of the front kick because, by this means, the technique is made to miss but the defender is left close enough to make use of any openings which may present themselves.

A circular kick cannot be countered effectively by stepping to the side since either the defender will move into the technique and increase its force or he will move in its direction and be caught anyway. In this case, it is better to step into the attack, so the foot curves harmlessly around the back, leaving the attacker standing helplessly on one leg. A step back can also be used together with timing, so an immediate counter can be launched.

The usage of body movements to avoid attacks is known as *tai sabaki*. It is best accompanied by a deflection block or a guard of some kind, in case the thwarted attacker lashes out wildly.

Timing is also very important when using a block. When an attack is launched, it starts at zero speed and builds to its maximum as the target is approached. If it misses, there is a little time when it is being slowed down and recovered. Both the pre- and post-attack intervals are known as 'dead time'. During dead time, the attack is generating little kinetic energy and may be countered with less risk.

For this reason, many ryu advise closing quickly with the attacker and blocking his techniques at source. The strong defender will stand firmly in sanchin stance and block powerfully. The less strong will use body evasion linked with deflection blocks to achieve the same result. The same block can be used either directly or as a deflection.

Closing quickly has another benefit. If someone swings a pole, maximum impact energy is developed at the tip and any attempt to apply a block there may cause injury. Near the grip, however, there is less energy and a block applied there will prove safer.

The Japanese word for block is *uke*.

The Head Block

The head block can be used as a deflection or as a power block that numbs the attacker's arm on impact. Whichever is chosen, the blocking shoulder must not rise, otherwise its strength is lost. The blocking elbow must not stand out from the side of the body or the effective range of the block is diminished. Also the elbow must not be higher than the hand or only a weak deflection can be achieved.

Head block works best from a close distance, moving inside the attack to where maximum force is not being generated. To practise it, the karateka takes up left or right forward stance and blocks with the appropriate arm. For best effect, the block should always be performed using the same arm as the forward leg. The blocking arm is bent at the elbow and drives diagonally upwards across the front of the chest. The knuckles of the fist are directed forwards. As the elbow reaches maximum height, the forearm is strongly rotated so the little finger comes to lie uppermost. This causes the bones of the forearm to be protected by muscle. In a power block, the forearm is conditioned to withstand impact and the bone used to block the attack.

The forearm twist must be strong since it snaps the block into its final shape. An incoming punch is met by the rising forearm and redirected over the karateka's head (**figure 49**).

There are two variants of this block. The non-blocking arm can first be extended and then pulled back strongly as the block is made. This pull-through is characteristic of Shotokan and produces a very strong technique. The other variant advises against blocking so close to the body and argues that a miscalculation can prove damaging. It prefers to interrupt the path of the incoming punch closer to source and drives the block diagonally forward as well as up. The elbow is bent and the forearm held well away from the body. This latter form, encountered in Wado ryu, gives a more gradual deflection and allows stronger blows to be diverted with less energy.

The forearm is not held horizontal unless power blocking. The average head block offers an angled surface, deflecting the punch to one side.

The Japanese name for head block is *jodan uke*.

Figure 49 Head block: the rising forearm redirects an oncoming punch

X-block

X-block, or *juji uke*, can be used both as a head and a lower body block. It is a particularly strong block but suffers from the disadvantage of using both arms in its execution, leaving none for a quick follow-up. To practise x-block against a head attack, the karateka takes up forward stance and, as the opponent punches to the face, both elbows bend and the forearms cross in front of and out from the chest. The arms continue to rise diagonally and outwards, with palms facing to the sides. As the block reaches maximum height, the forearms are quickly rotated and the palms turn forwards and down. The attacker's punch is caught at the wrist in the 'V' formed by the defender's hands.

The block may be performed with the hands open or closed. The open hands can be used to grab the attacker's trapped arm and pull it down.

As with the head block, it is important not to let the elbows move to the side of the body, nor let them rise higher than the blocking hands.

The lower block is more dangerous and requires that the hands be pulled into fists to avoid damage to fingers. It is used against front kicks but is an unsatisfactory technique in many ways. The downwards scissors action of the block can bring the defender's face too close to the attacker's fists for comfort. Also if a front kick is abruptly checked with x-block, it can drop quickly to the floor and the attacker is able to follow with a face punch. The defender's arms are too low to retrieve and his face is left unguarded and thrust out.

While it is customary to x-block a low kick from forward stance, this is not to be recommended for the reasons given above. It is much better to block with a straight back and bent knees, one locking into the back of the other to provide rigidity. This application is seen in the kata *heian* (pinan) *godan*. The upright stance and even weight distribution allows the defender to quickly withdraw if necessary.

The same blocking movement is used in both lower and head block.

Outer Block

Outer block can be used to deflect attacks to the head (*jodan*) or body (*chudan*). The blocking surface is the little finger or the 'outer' side of the forearm. The angle between the upper arm and the lower is 90 degrees; when blocking a head punch, the upper arm is horizontal and the forearm is vertical. For blocking a midsection punch, the right angle is maintained and the fist is held at shoulder height but well across the body.

Outer block can be practised while advancing forwards or retreating backwards. The most common form of practice uses forward stance. The karateka steps from left forward to right forward stance and, during the movement, his right arm bends at the elbow so the fist is pointing vertically upwards (**figure 50**). The blocking arm tends to trail behind the body during the step, causing tension across the chest muscles. As the right foot sets down, the blocking forearm is swept across the body and, as full weight comes down on the leading leg, the block completes with a muscle spasm that makes the whole body strong enough to withstand an impact (**figure 51**).

The Shotokan school use pull-through to generate additional force and extend the non-blocking left arm forward with the fist unclenched. As weight is brought down onto the right foot, the left arm is strongly withdrawn.

The beginner must take care not to turn the upper body into the block, since this removes the chance of quickly using the uninvolved arm to deliver a counter. Also, he must keep the blocking elbow and wrist in one plane. If the wrist leads, as is common with novices, the block loses power and will not check a strong attack. If the block stops too soon, the attack will be displaced but not miss entirely. Therefore it is important not to check the block until it has swung as far as the opposite shoulder.

Outer block (to the mid-section) is known as *chudan soto uke*.

Inner Block

Inner block is a more difficult technique to use than either head block or outer block. It can be used to protect the head or mid-section and uses the inner edge, or thumb-side, of the forearm. As with outer block, the upper and forearm are held at a 90 degree angle, regardless of whether a head- or mid-section application is used. Though it too can be practised from any stance,

Figure 50 The first stage of an outer block: the shoulders swing wide

Figure 51 Completing an outer block so the punch is deflected well to the side

Figure 52 The first stage of an inner block, preparatory to 'pull-back'

Figure 53 Inner block: completing the pull-back and swinging out the block

it is customary to use forward stance for basic training.

From left forward stance, the karateka steps into right stance. As he does so, his right arm moves across the stomach with knuckles facing upwards (**figure 52**). The arm is then swept up and across the front of the chest like a windscreen wiper, coming to a halt in front of the right shoulder as the stance change is completed (**figure 53**). As the block completes, the knuckles suddenly rotate so the large knuckles of the index and middle finger are facing forwards. Much of the power for this block comes from the hips.

In Shotokan, the non-blocking left arm is extended forwards and pulled back vigorously as the block is made. This produces a stronger technique and ensures that the upper body does not turn too far by balancing the action of the hips.

Beginners usually got the sequence wrong, leaving everything until the last split second and then hurrying it. They also tend to block too close to the body, forgetting the 90 degree bend at the elbow. The Japanese term for inner block (to midsection) is *chudan uchi uke*.

Augmented Forearm Block
Augmented forearm block is an inner or outer block using the non-blocking arm to add power and rigidity to the technique. It can be employed for mid-section or head attacks and is effective from any stance. It is at its strongest when delivered from forward stance and most clearly seen in the outer block configuration.

From left forward stance, the karateka advances and allows both arms to fall to the left hip. As weight is put on to the front leg, both arms simultaneously swing up and outwards. At the moment of impact, the body is tightened to absorb shock. The right arm is arranged as a typical 90-degree outer block and the left arm is brought across the lower chest, close to it. The left fist

Figure 54 Knife block, showing the left arm ready for pull-back

finishes palm up at the right elbow.

Swinging both arms at speed creates a more powerful block which utilizes the power developed by the stomach and hips.

The Japanese term for augmented block is *morote uke*.

Knife Block

Knife block (*shuto uke*) is an effective technique, though less powerful than the closed fist blocks described earlier. It can be used in many ways but the most common is an outwards cut with a palm-forwards delivery of the blocking hand. There is a divergence of opinion on how the block should be applied. The Shotokan use it in a shallow cutting action that interrupts the attacking punch near source. Wado ryu, in contrast, uses a vertical palm-forward knife block that catches the punch near the wrist, making it easier to deflect. Shito ryu uses a thrusting strike of the knife hand that is direct rather than circular. Kyokushinkai uses a large circular movement that is more chopping than cutting in action.

Knife block is best practised from cat or back stance. The karateka starts in left and steps forwards into right stance. The right hand reaches across and makes as though to cup the left ear (**figure 54**). The left hand extends forwards and down. As weight is put on the right leg, the right arm cuts forwards while the left withdraws strongly to the centre of the chest. At the last

Figure 55 Completing a knife block; other arm withdrawn to chest

minute, the blocking knife hand twists palm forwards, giving an added snap to the technique (**figure 55**).

A completed right knife block has a right angle bend at the elbow and the tips of the fingers just above the height of the right shoulder. The blocking palm is facing forwards and downwards and the other is palm upwards, fingers extended and resting against the centre of the chest.

It is possible also to do an augmented knife block, trailing both arms to the left during the step. The right arm still cups the left ear but the left trails downwards and behind. As the new stance is adopted, both swing rapidly up and across the body, finishing in the usual position but utilizing the power generated by both arms.

A knife block which contacts the attacker's forearm can hook around and draw it down. This ploy is most effective when used against a mid-section punch since the draw-down uses the stomach muscles and not those of the shoulders.

When stepping back from a punch, it is also possible to cut inwards with the knife hand, so that the palm is turned to the face. In this case, the person stepping back from left back stance will extend their left arm, palm open and down-turned. The right is taken out and back with the palm facing forwards as though saluting. As the left arm is pulled back, the right arm swings across the body, rather like the outer block. At the last moment, the blocking knife hand twists palm towards the face and the left simultaneously turns palm upwards.

Ridge Hand Block
Ridge hand block uses the thumb side of the knife hand configuration in a blocking-type movement. It can be practised from either back or cat stance and is best shown while stepping back from an attacker. The right arm is taken across the chest, palm against the ribs. The left hand extends palm down and forwards, as in the knife block. As the left arm is withdrawn, the right arcs up like a windscreen wiper and, at the last instant, turns palm upwards. Once the block has been made, the wrist is rotated so a grab can follow. The grab uses the thumb, third, fourth and fifth fingers. The index finger is left outstretched along the captured forearm.

It is usual to curl the back of the hand over the attacker's forearm as a precaution to delay its retrieval.

Palm Heel and Wrist Blocks
Palm heel block is a short-range technique employed from cat or back stance. It is a deflection and not a power block, using a slapping motion to knock a punch off course. The elbow is kept close to the body and the fingers of the blocking hand are extended or slightly curled. The block crosses the body in the manner of a reverse knife hand and deflects the technique close to its target.

The back of the wrist can be used to divert a punch when used with body movement. For example, if the attacker lunges forwards with a mid-section punch, the defender can step back with the front foot into a narrow straddle stance. During the step back, the forward arm extends and contacts the incoming punch at the wrist. The back of the deflecting hand hooks over the attacker's fist and, using the hip energy of the forming stance, deflects it past the front of the body.

The bent wrist (*koken*) is useful for knocking an attacker's fist upwards. This is a close-range block better suited to deflecting a grab than a punch.

Lower Block
Lower block, or *gedan barai*, is a powerful down-sweeping technique that works well against a kick. The block's action must be properly formed so it meets the incoming technique at an angle and redirects it. A careless lower block can bring the lighter bones of the forearm into vicious contact with those of the leg in an unequal contest. The most powerful lower blocks are developed during a turn, though they can also be practised from forward stance.

From ready stance, the karateka steps back with his right foot into left forward stance. At the same time, he extends his right arm, fist closed, in a steep downward angle in front of the groin. The left arm folds up and across the chest, with the little finger of the closed fist touching the right collarbone. As the stance is completing, the right arm quickly pulls back to the hip and the left swings down in an arc, the elbow gradually straightening until, at the lowest point, it becomes straight. During the block, the fist rotates little finger side outwards. The block is made with the hammer fist, or with the outside edge of the forearm.

In the completed block, the left arm reaches out and down, finishing a couple of inches above the left knee and slightly to the outside of it.

The attacker's leg should be contacted as the elbow is three-quarters straight. It can then be safely batted to one side.

Outer Sweeping Block

Outer sweep, or *soto harai uke*, is a deflection block that scoops under the attacker's kick and either traps it or knocks it to one side (**figures 56, 57**). It is used in conjunction with body evasion and hip-twist. From left fighting stance, the karateka steps to the outside with his front leg and twists his hips clockwise. This causes the upper body to swivel and the leading arm to swing around and up in a hooking or slapping motion. Although experienced karateka perform this block with open hands, the novice is strongly advised to close his fist. If timing is wrong, the fingers can get caught and bent back by the lifting kick.

The block is made with the forearm.

Inner Sweeping Block

Inner sweeping block, or *uchi harai uke*, resembles a lower block but is executed together with a body movement (**figures 58, 59**). From left fighting stance, the defender steps back and diagonally outwards with his right leg. The body leans away in the direction of the step and the left foot is withdrawn a little way. The left arm sweeps downwards, knocking the kick outwards. As with outer sweeping block, the hands should be closed to avoid injury. The diagonal step back causes the opponent's kick to miss and a light push produces a substantial deflection.

Figure 56 Outer sweep: forward arm preparing to scoop under the kick

Figure 57 The shoulders rotate and the oncoming kick is caught

Figure 58 Inner sweep uses pull-back to power it

Figure 59 The hips rotate strongly away from the block

CHAPTER 7: DEVELOPING FORCE IN KARATE

For an impact technique to be effective, it must hit the right target with the right technique and the right degree of force. The force may be generated by obvious muscle action or it may come from an apparently relaxed and unfocused technique. The former corresponds to the hard or *wai chia* styles of Shaolin woshu and the latter to the soft or *nei chia* styles of Wudang. Since the majority of all karate comes from Shaolin, then it follows that karate is basically a hard style of fighting.

It is easier to teach the principles of hardness, relying as they do on definable physical actions such as hip-twist and muscle spasm, but that does not mean they are in any way superior. It is said that the Shaolin forms were only a pre-training for the more effective soft school. Certainly in wushu circles, the harmless looking tai chi chuan is reckoned to be the most effective of all fighting systems.

Some soft techniques are taught in karate but they are rudimentary and little understood.

The Focus

The principle of the hard technique lies in its focus, or *kime*. Focus is where the maximum energy of a technique is concentrated. Since it is obvious that a punch cannot continue accelerating indefinitely, then maximum acceleration must be achieved in the instant before contact. The limb has a finite length and acceleration must therefore reach its peak near full extension. This combination of acceleration and distance produces a peak of power at one point – the point of focus.

A focused technique has little leeway, so if the opponent moves suddenly, maximum power is not delivered on impact and it becomes 'unfocused'.

The Principles of Power Development

The effect produced by an impact strike is due to the kinetic energy it possesses. Upon impact, this energy is passed to the target. If the transfer is rapid, there is a jolting shock; if slow, a violent push results.

The first requirement for any body weapon is that of mass. The greater the mass, the more force it is capable of generating. The second requirement is acceleration. In order to develop force, the weapon mass must be accelerated to as high a velocity as possible. A slow-moving but massive body develops a great deal of energy. The same energy can be generated by a smaller mass but the velocity on impact must be many times greater. It is therefore important that smaller-boned people concentrate on developing as much speed as possible.

When the speeding fist or foot hits the target, it gives up its energy in an instant, producing a tremendous shock. Action equals reaction, giving the theoretical result that the target flies backwards with an equivalent force to that applied. In practice, a great amount of energy is shed in recoil – that backwards pulse of energy caused by the target not yielding quickly enough. Recoil must be minimized by making the weapon as fast-moving, massive or as rigid as possible, so the impact energy takes the path of lesser resistance into the opponent. There are two ways this can be achieved: one by anchoring the attacking stance firmly to the ground and the other by making the blow heavier.

In the first way, the stance is used to resist recoil by ensuring the weapon is locked rigid on impact. If a kick, the leg must be fully straightened and, if a punch, the elbow must lock out. If this is not done, recoil can cause the knee or elbow to bend and act as a shock absorber. There must be a lot of weight directed forwards and anchored there by a prop. In the case of a punch, this prop is the fully straightened rear leg. A bent back leg can give way under recoil. The upper body must lean in behind the punch so it cannot be pushed back and maximum weight must be brought to bear on the front leg, otherwise it can rise. This can be achieved by bearing forward until the knee comes over the toes.

The kick cannot utilize this method since it is impossible to resist substantial recoil while standing on one leg. Kick techniques use the second alternative, which is that of increasing body weight.

It is a fact that the moving body possesses energy, even when travelling at constant speed. This energy is called momentum. Passengers in a car tend to continue moving at the same speed when the driver jams on the brakes, and it is momentum which drives them hard into the safety belts. Momentum makes the body feel as though it weighs more. If, during a punch or kick, the body is moved behind the blow, that blow seems more powerful. This is because the moving body acts as an energy buffer, reducing recoil by increasing the weight of the weapon.

During kicks, the mass of the leg is accelerated and then augmented by swivelling the hips behind it. A slight forwards hop on the supporting leg at the moment of impact transfers body weight forwards and makes even a one-legged stance seem stable.

This can be extrapolated to punches and a high and non-rigid stance can absorb recoil if the body is moving behind it. High-energy punches can be delivered from any stance, not necessarily one that is rigid, and this realization has led to a greater fluidity in the practice of karate.

A focused technique must, by its very nature, be accurately targeted. It is, after all, a sledgehammer blow which represents the maximum impact power capable of being generated by that person. The range is critical since all the various components needed to make it an effective strike will come together at one point in space. A technique which is focused for its maximum effect deep inside the opponent's body will not achieve that goal. Such a punch, for example, will not be at its maximum speed on first contact yet, as soon as it touches, kinetic energy is shed very quickly and maximum speed becomes no longer attainable. To further complicate matters, the recoil-reducing body movement is used too late. It is therefore necessary to focus on the surface of the target and try to deliver as much shock power as possible. Should the target move back, the punch will reach its maximum power short of it and prove ineffective even if it makes contact.

The act of focusing a technique can actually weaken it if done wrongly. If the whole body is to become rigid at the moment of impact, a finite time is needed for the muscles to act and so they begin to tighten just before impact. This has a pronounced braking effect on the punch and robs it of kinetic energy.

When attacking soft areas, such as the stomach, it is as well to use unfocused punches. These do not tighten on impact since there is less recoil to contend with. Like the focused strike, they use body movement but aim at deep penetration rather than a sharp impact. This is achieved through a greater degree of body movement than is found in the focused techniques. The unfocused technique is accelerated as strongly but there is no attempt to tighten the body on impact. The best examples of powerful and unfocused strikes are those delivered with a swinging or hooking motion such as roundhouse punch (*mawashi zuki*), hook punch (*kage zuki*) and close punch (*ura zuki*).

The *kiai* is used during a focused technique. It manifests itself as a violent exhaltation of air in the form of a shout, made just before or during a committed attack. The kiai originates from the diaphragm and muscles of the lower chest and stomach. These strongly contract, forcing air out of the lungs and adding sharpness to the technique. Additionally, kiai strengthens the body and makes it that much more able to absorb a blow without injury.

High-energy Punching (Figure 60)
The easiest technique to practise with first is the reverse punch, since it incorporates all the principles encountered in high energy punching. The karateka starts in left fighting stance by leaning back on the right foot and extending the left hand. The right hand is held open and pulled back behind the right hip. The forward hand starts to withdraw and the hips rotate so they are fully forwards facing. The shoulders are left twisted to the right and a tension builds up in the muscles of the back. When this reaches a peak, the shoulders are released and whip around behind the hips. Weight is quickly transferred to the front leg and the right arm thrusts past the right side as the left arm is being withdrawn.

As the right arm reaches the limit of travel, the hand closes into a fist and rotates palm down. At the moment of impact, the right arm is virtually straight and travelling at its highest speed. The left arm has been pulled back to the left hip and tightly closed and body movement is putting weight over the front leg.

The hip-twist puts stress on the muscles of the back and these throw the punching shoulder forwards. This action is strengthened by the withdrawal of the other arm. The closing of both fists on impact adds rigidity and the forward body movement soaks up recoil.

It is also possible to punch strongly off the front fist by using pull-back of the non-punching arm. From left stance the karateka moves his right hand forwards, around and back in a small circle. As it is withdrawn,

Figure 60 High-energy punching

the right shoulder is drawn back and the left thrust forward. As this happens, the left fist is thrown at the opponent and both fists tighten up on impact. Both hip and shoulder on the punching side twist forwards and weight is put on the forward knee to increase rigidity.

The punch can be considerably strengthened if delivered during an actual step. A short step, either with the leading leg drawing out the stance or with a rear foot stepping through, can add considerably to impact.

High-energy Kicking (Figure 61)
Kicks can be strengthened by bringing the body strongly behind them. The muscles of the upper leg snap out front kick and this action can be strengthened by either swivelling the hips behind it, or by thrusting them forwards in the direction of the kick. In conjunction with the former method, a hop on the supporting leg is effective in adding still more power. It is a good idea to lift the hips behind the kick by raising up on the ball of the supporting leg as the kick impacts. The raising of the hips contributes more power than is lost by recoil through the raised heel. When moving the hips forward, it is important not to lean backwards since this can destabilize the kick and cause loss of balance. Both methods work by throwing weight forwards at the last minute and gaining a kind of dynamic, if short-lived, stability.

Increasing the power of the turning kick requires shoulder action that winds up the spine, adding power to the hip-twist. From left stance, the karateka leans

Figure 61 High-energy kicking

and twists his body to the left. The right leg lifts and the hips swivel in the direction of the upper body. The hip of the kicking leg actually rolls up and above that of the supporting leg. The kicking knee is raised and snaps out while the body is in a 'T' shape, with the supporting leg forming the upright, one side being the kicking leg and the other the body which leans back in line with the outstretched leg. The back must be arched during delivery, otherwise recoil can cause loss of balance.

Side kicks are strengthened by using either the one-step variant described later, or by hopping forwards on the supporting leg just before impact.

Short-range power

In close-up confrontations, there may not be the distance in which to accelerate a technique. In this situation it is necessary to use the power which can be developed by suddenly tightening all the body's muscles. When someone is tickled, they jerk spasmodically and, for an instant, the body becomes rigid. This jerk is actually quite powerful and can be used both to accelerate a short-range technique and soak up recoil.

To practise it, the karateka stands in a high stance, such as natural or semi-forward stance. If the left leg is forwards, the left arm leads and vice versa. The leading arm pulls back and, at the same time, the punching arm moves forward. There is a short step forward by either leg and, as the punch touches, the body locks up. If the spasm is sharp enough, the blow will have a surprising amount of power. There is no need to twist the wrist on impact.

CHAPTER 8: THE BASIC TECHNIQUES OF KARATE

Basic techniques are the essential building blocks of karate, from which expertise, competence and effectiveness derive. They break down the flowing sequences of the expert into individual component parts, allowing the student to practise on one easily assimilated part at a time. Basic techniques are therefore single kicks, punches or strikes, each of which may be further broken down into its component parts.

This modular arrangement is both an advantage and a disadvantage. Originally, small numbers of students closely copied the Master as he went through a series of movements. Many movements had no names and the students often did not understand their purpose until much later. The advantage of this is that it teaches students to think in terms of several movements, one running into the next. The disadvantage is that it works only under close scrutiny, where everyone's smallest mistake is quickly detected and corrected. This method requires small classes.

As karate became more popular and classes increased in size, it became necessary to seek alternative methods of teaching. Unlike the flowing movements of aikido and jiu jitsu, the individual movements of karate could be isolated and taught as basic techniques. Each part of a technique could be performed to a count and, by this means, a large class could be controlled by one teacher.

Unfortunately, modular teaching can seriously impede the natural flow of techniques and encourage the student to think in terms of consecutive action. The karateka applying basic techniques will see the attacker's punch approaching, block it and then follow the block with a counter. The experienced karateka can achieve this in an instant of time but, even so, the system remains limited.

A teaching system grounded in the study of basic techniques does not lend itself to a concurrent approach. The latter requires that an approaching punch be blocked and in the same movement the counter-attack be launched. Concurrent systems are intrinsically faster and more effective but can only be taught by the old method.

Training up to black belt in karate involves the

Figure 62 Lunge punch, beginning from forward stance

sequential method of teaching. After that, the concurrent system can be used. This is because the skilled student has mastered basic techniques and need not spend time concentrating on how to get one part of a whole concurrent movement right. He is able to faithfully copy the whole, his knowledge of the individual parts coming automatically.

Correctly taught karate is therefore a very advanced training system, combining the ability to teach modular techniques to a large number of students with that of being able to demonstrate concurrent techniques to a smaller number of advanced students.

Practical Basic Techniques

Lunge punch

The lunge punch (*oizuki* or *junzuki*) is, as its name implies, a punch which uses the momentum of a moving body to generate power and reduce recoil. The punch is delivered with the same forward leg and fist. Therefore, if the left foot is forwards, the left fist will be also. The technique is that of an advancing punch where impact is timed to coincide with the limit of the body's forward movement.

It is important to synchronize the technique's components properly, so the punch occurs when it is supposed to, and not an instant too early or too late. If the punch is released too early, it impedes the body's forward progress and produces a jerky delivery. Because the body has not fully closed range, the early punch will tend to land short. Conversely, punching too late means that the body has actually stopped moving when the punch impacts. This means that the body's reservoir of momentum has been lost and only that of the fist remains. The technique is thus seriously weakened.

Correct delivery occurs when the front foot is settling into its new position. First the ball of the foot settles, then the heel, and it is during the latter that the punch is timed to impact.

Lunge punch begins from an existing forward stance (**figure 62**), or it may be generated by the karateka stepping back from ready stance with his right foot and sweeping the left arm down and across the body in left *gedan barai*. From this stance, the rear foot is shifted forwards, sliding past the front foot (**figure 63**) and continuing to advance on a full pace. Only the ball of the advancing foot rests on the floor and no weight is placed upon it at this time. The previously extended arm is left out during the step and is only withdrawn as the new punching arm extends (**figure 64**). Beginners commonly withdraw the front arm as they step and this must be avoided. It is also important to keep the

Figure 63 Stepping through with the rear leg

Figure 64 Pulling back the leading hand and simultaneously punching

supporting leg bent so height remains constant, with no bobbing up and down.

As the step reaches its limit, body weight begins to shift forward and the heel begins to drop. Immediately, the extended arm is forcefully pulled back while the punching arm drives outwards. As the heel settles to the floor, the back leg stiffens and straightens and the punch rotates palm down on impact. The whole body tenses into *zenkutsu dachi*, to absorb recoil.

Since lunge punch is a basic technique, it can be safely left extended and not pulled back until the next advance. It can be delivered to any target on the head or body, though care should be taken to adjust the degree of rotation of the fist to suit the angle being used. Punches to the head are called *jodan*, to the mid-section, *chudan*, and to the groin, *gedan*.

It is customary to practise lunge punch in conjunction with turn/head block (*jodan uke*). Therefore, in preparation for the turn, the karateka first looks over his shoulder to check what he is turning into. If it is clear, he slides his back foot across and twists the hips (**figures 65, 66**). As this happens, the extended fist is drawn back and folded at the elbow, forming a shield. The other fist crosses it at the forearm, making what is virtually an x-block. As the turn completes, the originally extended arm is forcibly withdrawn and the other rises up and forwards, across and away from the face (**figure 67**). As the block concludes, the back leg is locked straight and all the muscles of the body tighten in anticipation of impact.

During lunge-punch practice, care must be taken to preserve the forward stance in its correct form. The back leg must not bend at the knee, the stance width must be maintained and the front knee come to rest above the instep. The hips und shoulders must be kept square on.

Reverse punch
Reverse punch, or *gyakuzuki*, is one of the commonest karate techniques. It is so named because, unlike lunge punch, the opposite fist to front leg is extended. Reverse punch is effective while advancing, retreating or just standing still. It uses the hips rather more than lunge punch and, to facilitate this, the stance is specialized. Some schools of karate favour a direct step from one reverse-punch stance to another, but the more traditional use a semi-circular step. During it, stance height must remain constant and the leading fist not wag about.

As with *oizuki*, the punch is released only when weight is coming down on the new leading foot. The body moves behind the punch and considerable

Figure 65 Preparing for the turn/head block from lunge punch stance

Figure 66 Practising a turn/head block: drawing the fist back to form a shield

momentum is developed. This must be harnessed to the energy produced in the punching arm by correct timing. The back leg straightens on impact, giving an extra shove to the fist as it impacts.

From the basic lower block/forward stance used for lunge punch, the hips first wind back slightly. Sometimes this is associated with a slight raising of the body. The hips then twist forward but the shoulders remain pulled back for an instant. This sets up a torsion in the spine which is released when the shoulders swing to follow the hips. As the hips twist, the back leg swivels so its toes point straight ahead. Simultaneously the leading arm withdraws. This helps swing the shoulders behind the punch, which extends at exactly the same rate the non-punching arm is withdrawn. Just before impact, both fists rotate with the punching fist turning palm down and the withdrawn fist turning palm up.

The advancing reverse-punch technique begins from an existing stance (**figure 68**) achieved as above. The karateka steps forward with the rear leg and places it, sole down, in its new position. During this movement, the hips open out and the reverse punch is cocked (**figure 69**, overleaf) ready for use. When stepping, stance width must be retained. The beginner often brings his front foot in as well as forwards and ends up being unstable. Where there is a circular step, the rear foot pulls in, alongside and away from the supporting foot. The beginner often takes his advancing foot too far to the side, opening his stance to groin kick. Constant height must be maintained throughout and the outstretched arm should not waver. As weight sinks onto the heel, the punch is released (figure 70, overleaf).

The turn from reverse punch is usually associated with a lower block (*gedan barai*). The karateka first looks over his shoulder to confirm all is clear, then he slides his rear foot across and well behind the front foot. Once the moving foot has settled in its final position, the hips begin to turn but the shoulders are held back an instant, to allow torsion to build up in the spine. They are then released and the upper torso swivels to face the new direction.

The blocking arm is the one currently extended at the time of the turn (**figure 71**, overleaf). As the shoulders begin twisting around, the blocking arm is bent at the elbow and the little finger side of the fist contacts the chest. Those schools which use pull-through will extend the non-blocking arm at this point (**figure 72**, overleaf). As the body continues to turn, the blocking arm sweeps down and across it, strengthened by the pull back of the non-blocking arm. Weight is transferred onto the new front leg and the body tightens to withstand impact (**figure 73**, overleaf).

Figure 67 Practising a turn/head block: completing the turn/head block

Figure 68 Beginning the advancing reverse punch

Figure 69 Stepping through with the reverse punch cocked and ready for use

Figure 70 The hips and body weight drive forward

Novices often step too far across as they turn and this produces a short stance with exaggerated side step, vulnerable to a groin kick counter. If there is insufficient step across, the resultant stance is narrow and unstable. During the turn, the stance must be maintained at the correct height. The blocking arm must not be swung out too wide of the body, but should come to a complete stop just above and to the outside of the leading knee.

Front kick

Front kick (*maegeri*) uses the ball of the foot to penetrate deeply into the opponent. It exists in a number of forms, all of which rely on contraction of the muscles of the upper leg to accelerate the knee to a position where the kick can be safely delivered. The knee determines the height of the kick. The speed at which it is raised will determine, together with other factors, the force of the kick. In all forms of maegeri, it is very important to retrieve the kick after use. This is done by snapping the kicking leg out and back before setting it down once more.

Beginners tend to be unbalanced when practising front kick. The weight of the leg swinging forward pulls the upper body behind it and balance is lost. The unbalanced kick thumps down heavily on the floor and there is little possibility of avoiding a waiting counter. Some novices try to compensate for this by leaning away from the direction of the kick. When kicking against no resistance, such as the air, this solution can work, but

Figure 71 The blocking arm extended during the turn from reverse punch

Figure 72 Using pull-through during a turning lower block

against a kicking bag, recoil drives the karateka backwards and out of balance.

The trick is to keep the body weight over the supporting leg and lean back only slightly to counter the leg's momentum. This lean-back should not be so great as to take the head past an imaginary vertical line rising from the heel of the supporting leg. For extra stability, the arms must be kept close to the body and the supporting leg bent. Novices have a tendency to bob up and down as they advance through a series of kicks.

The short-range front kick is the easiest one to start with, since it uses virtually only leg movement. In order to have distance in which to accelerate, it is always advisable to kick with the back leg from either a forward or a fighting stance. Both of these have the necessary hip position and weight distribution to allow rapid deployment. From left fighting stance, the guard is maintained with the left fist leading and at the same height as the shoulder. The elbow is bent at a right-angle and the arm is taken across the mid-line of the body. The forward guard should not be so low that techniques to the chest and chin can slip in over it; neither should it be so high as to allow access to good body punches, or make it liable to be knocked back into the face. The right arm is kept to the side, with the elbow held in and the fist lying palm-up against the belt.

The guard is stationary as the right knee swings forward and up. As the knee reaches its final height, it

Figure 73 The blocking arm sweeps down at the conclusion of lower block

brakes to a rapid stop and the lower leg is released to shoot out and strike the target. As the lower leg is reaching its maximum range, it is snapped back and finally lowered to the floor in its original position.

It is possible to use only a little hip action behind the kick because the supporting leg does not swivel. The technique should be practised until it is possible to either step back from the kick or advance with it. If the kick is set down in front of the supporting leg, the guard must be changed so the same hand and foot lead upon landing.

The mid-range front kick either uses hip-twist, or the supporting heel lifts to deliver it. Either fighting stance or forward stance can be used and, if the latter, then both fists should be at shoulder height, with elbows bent 90 degrees (**figure 74**). If fighting stance is chosen (**figure 75**) the guard must be changed during the early stages of an advancing kick delivery (**figure 76**) so, when it sets down, the guard is correct. As the knee rises, the bent supporting leg swivels and the toes point outwards (**figure 77**).

Figure 74 Forward stance used to deliver the mid-range front kick

The supporting foot reaches the limit of its rotation as the kick lands on the target. Not only does this add torsional energy to the kick's power, it also substantially increases range. This can be easily demonstrated with the aid of a partner. The karatcka faces his partner and, keeping his hips facing directly forward, performs a slow right front kick. The partner positions himself slightly out of range, so the kick does not quite reach. Then the kick is repeated but, this time, the karateka twists outwards on his supporting leg. He will find he can now reach his opponent.

Extra range can also be achieved if the supporting leg drags a short distance during the kick's delivery. The drag must occur instants before the foot lands on its target. This forward movement of body weight both reduces recoil and increases range.

Long-range front kick is achieved by means of a scissors step from either forward or fighting stance (**figure 78**). The guard is maintained during the step and novices must take care not to flap their elbows away from the body. Properly done, the scissors stance (**figure 79**) can provide a bonus in initial acceleration of the kick. The length of the step must, however, be carefully judged. Too long a step can reduce range to the point where full power and speed are no longer possible. Too short a step will leave the kick out of range and give a reduced bonus in initial acceleration of the technique.

From fighting stance, the rear foot slides forwards and is set down with the toes turned outwards. The rear leg lifts off and accelerates to the correct height, before braking to a stop and snapping out the lower

Figure 75 Fighting stance may also be used to deliver the mid-range front kick

Figure 76 Raising the knee and maintaining the guard

Figure 77 Driving the kick out by straightening the knee

Figure 78 Starting long-range front kick from fighting stance

Figure 79 Using a scissors step to increase acceleration

leg (**figure 80**). The kick is retrieved and set gently down, ball of foot first.

Roundhouse kick
Roundhouse kick (*mawashigeri*) uses either the ball of the foot or the instep as weapons. The former is more powerful but has a slightly shorter range than the latter. It is called a 'roundhouse' or 'turning' kick because, during delivery, the foot does not travel straight but rather describes a circular path, rising up from the ground and then continuing in an arc to the target. During the final part of its travel, it is parallel with the ground. The kick requires a great deal of hip movement to execute properly and can be delivered successfully with the front foot.

To practise front foot roundhouse, back or cat stance should be used (**figure 81**). Both of these favour a rapid movement of the front leg without disturbing the balance. The kicking knee is raised to the correct height and the supporting leg swivels as it does during a front kick (**figure 82**). The leg rotates a great deal further in a roundhouse kick because, on completion, the body is turned fully sideways on. When it is three-quarters turned away, the lower foot lashes out with toes either pointing (**figure 83**) or pulled back to allow impact with the ball of the foot.

As with front kick, there are two phases in power delivery. The first is when the kicking knee accelerates to the correct height and the second is when the lower foot is driven out. Hip-twist adds both power and range to the technique and also allows the body to lean away from counter-attack. Leaning back makes it easier to retain balance.

Roundhouse kick off the rear leg is more powerful because there is a greater distance in which it can accelerate. The hips turn further, allowing greater range, more power and a better lean-away of the upper body. The first stage in practising it is to lean the upper body, twisting it like an airplane turning and banking away. This puts a torsional stress on the spine which is relieved when the kicking leg lifts and the supporting leg begins to swivel (**figure 84**). As the knee accelerates to the correct height, the supporting leg continues to swivel until it has turned greater than a right angle. The kicking knee must move quickly across the front of the karateka's body where it acts as a bar against attacks.

Once the kick has been snapped out (**figure 85**), it is pulled back (**figure 86**, overleaf) and the body straightens to an upright position. As it is straightening, the supporting leg swivels back and the kicking leg is gently set down (**figure 87**, overleaf). The guard must be maintained throughout, so a quick defence can be made if

Figure 80 Concluding a long-range front kick. Note the fully extended kicking leg

Figure 81 A front-foot roundhouse kick, starting from cat stance

Figure 82 Front-foot roundhouse kick, showing the kicking leg raised to the correct height and hips rotating

Figure 83 The completion of a front-foot roundhouse kick: hips forward

Figure 84 Roundhouse kick off the rear legs: hips turn sideways on

Figure 85 The roundhouse kick is driven out

Figure 86 After completing the kick, the foot is quickly withdrawn

Figure 87 The kicking leg is set down and guard regained

the occasion warrants it.

Some schools of karate teach a form of roundhouse kick in which the body remains upright, even when kicking to the head. This requires supple hips to achieve the same degree of power and the torso is vulnerable to counter. On the other hand, it is a faster kick and leaves the user able to counter or press home his attack without having to first restore the body's equilibrium. It is not, however, a good idea to practise a kick in which the foot travels in a wide arc. This gives the opponent ample opportunity to take evasive action.

Full-contact schools teach a roundhouse kick which lifts almost vertically and travels to its target in a diagonal line. Whereas the classic roundhouse kick completes its travel parallel to the ground, this latter form does not, but goes directly to the target. It is more likely to catch elbows or shoulders, but is nevertheless extremely fast and powerful.

Novices should, as with all kicks, watch their balance. It is so very easy to lose balance, thumping down on the front leg afterwards. The arms must also be kept to the sides. Flailing them about diverts energy which could otherwise be channelled into the kick. A common fault is not to raise the knee high enough and then try to compensate by turning the hips too far and striking upwards with the side of the ankle.

The range of the kick can be increased by sliding forward on the supporting leg as the knee reaches correct height. This introduces the body's momentum in favour of the kick. Range can be further extended

Figure 88 Fighting stance is an uncommitted stance useful for delivering kicks

Figure 89 A scissors-step reduces distance and builds up acceleration

Figure 90 The kick is driven out strongly with the heel forwards

by means of a scissors step across the front leg (**figure 88**). It is important to turn the foot outwards as it sets down (**figure 89**), since this twists the hips into the correct position for a fast kick (**figure 90**). The length of the step should be adjusted to suit the circumstances. It is important not to bob up and down and the guard should be held firmly and correctly.

Side kick
Side kick (*yokogeri*) is a powerful straight kick that impacts primarily with the heel but also with the edge of the foot. It has a deceptively long range and is difficult to block. It is possible to practise side kick both from straddle and fighting stance.

From straddle stance (**figure 91**), the kicking leg is lifted and balance maintained by shifting body weight back over the supporting leg (**figure 92**, overleaf). Some schools lean back at the same time. The kicking knee is then straightened and driven heel-first into the target. During delivery, the supporting leg swivels and the body leans back, forming a 'Y' shape with the two legs (**figure 93**, overleaf). Afterwards, the foot is pulled back and the body once again assumes an upright position (**figure**

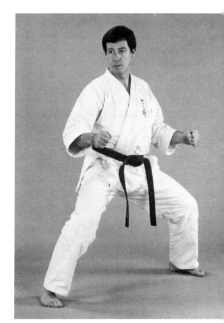

Figure 91 Straddle stance

Figure 92 Maintain balance by shifting the body weight back

Figure 93 The leg is fully straightened and the heel driven out

Figure 94 The front foot is quickly retrieved after a side kick

Figure 95 The conclusion of a side kick: the kicking foot resumes its original position

94) before it is set down in its original position (**figure 95**).

Beginners tend to slap the kicking foot down hard and, when this happens, it is evidence of poor balance. They tend also to set the spent kick directly down, without bringing the body upright first. The position of the arms must be checked to ensure they do not flap about during the kick. Getting the angle of the foot correct is perhaps the most difficult part. The foot is at right angles with the shin and the heel furthest out from the body. The sole is parallel with the floor. The foot position should be practised until it is possible to lift the big toe while depressing the others. Novices either kick with the soles of their feet or they fail to lock the foot in its correct angle.

One-step side kick can be extremely fast and powerful if the step is short and the kick used at just the right time to harness the considerable momentum generated. Experienced karateka hop sideways and aim to contact with the kick just as weight settles on the new front foot. A fast scissors step is used to advance in straddle stance. The passing foot can either slide in front of or behind (**figure 96**) the supporting leg (**figure 97**).

It is also possible to use side kick from fighting stance (**figure 98**), picking up the back leg and swivelling the

Figure 96 One step-side kick

Figure 97 The kicking leg is fully straightened

Figure 98 Side kick from fighting stance

Figure 99 The kicking leg is raised and brought forwards, the hips swivel square on

Figure 100 The kick is driven out

Figure 101 After the kick, the kicking leg is gently set down

hips to drive it forward. This is a complicated technique, requiring a deal of practice before it can be performed with any degree of competence. While maintaining the guard, the back foot is picked up and brought to the front (**figure 99**), as though for a normal front kick. The body is kept upright, the bent supporting leg swivels outwards and simultaneously the side kick is driven out. The upper body leans back and away from possible counter-attacks (**figure 100**). After the kick has landed, it is withdrawn and the correct upright stance readopted before setting down (**figure 101**).

The difficulty with this kick lies in the synchronizing of the hip-twist with the thrusting out of the kick. The purpose of the hip-twist is to provide impetus and it is therefore important that the kick is made while the hips are still turning. Many beginners turn and then kick, robbing the technique of a great deal of its power.

Side kick can also be used against the opponent's knee. The kicking foot is driven downwards onto the knee in a stamping motion. This particular kick is sometimes called *sokuto fumikomi*.

Figure 102 Left fighting stance prior to back kick

Figure 103 Maintaining the guard while rotating the body for a back kick

Back kick

There are various ways of performing back kick. The most common begins from fighting stance. By means of a strong hip-twist, the body is rotated so the back is turned towards the opponent. From left fighting stance (**figure 102**), the body swivels and weight is brought back and over the left supporting leg. The right leg is freed to move and slides in an arc, with the heel raised from the ground. The guard is maintained during the movement and the head turns with the body, so a clear view of the opponent can be maintained throughout (**figure 103**). The rotation of the body powers the kick and it is therefore important to kick while turning and not after the turn has stopped.

The heel is driven into the target (**figure 104**, overleaf) and withdrawn. As it is being pulled back, the turn continues until the karateka is once more facing forward (**figure 105**, overleaf). The foot is then gently set down (**figure 106**).

Beginners make many mistakes, most of which are associated with the turn. Before it can take place properly, body weight must be quickly transferred over the supporting leg. If this is not done, the turn will only go

Figure 104 Back kick: driving the heel into the target

Figure 105 Pulling back the heel after delivering a back kick

Figure 106 The hips have now rotated and the kicking leg is gently set down

so far and the following kick will be off-centre. Hip-twist during the turn must be extremely powerful, otherwise the kick will lack force. When the kick is withdrawn, the body must continue turning until square on, otherwise it will end up at a disadvantageous angle to the opponent. The elbows must be kept in during the kick and the head should be lifted up. The kick must drive out straight and not hook upwards.

One school of karate advocates a step to the inside with the front foot before launching the kick. While this is helpful in ensuring a proper set-up for the kick, it nevertheless involves an extra movement and can telegraph the technique. The same style is curious in that it advocates kicking blind, with the head turned away.

Reverse roundhouse kick
This is not a traditional karate technique but has been taken from the Korean analogue of *taekwondo*. It is a

high, circling kick which impacts with the heel, delivered by means of a back kick-type movement from fighting stance. The body is swivelled around quickly but, instead of driving the kick directly out, it is lifted and hooks with the heel at the back of the opponent's head (**figure 107**). Continued turning on the supporting leg plus the pull back of the spent kick returns the karateka to an upright and forward-facing position. To avoid injury while training, it is customary to point the toes and slap the target with the sole of the foot.

Reverse roundhouse is one of the most difficult kicks to do and requires a high degree of balance during the turn, otherwise the karateka can literally fall over. Recovery of the spent kick is also difficult and it is all too easy to slap the kicking foot down with no trace of pull-back. Such a landing leaves the karateka unable to respond to sudden attack.

Figure 107 Delivering a reverse roundhouse kick

CHAPTER 9: COMBINATION TECHNIQUES OF KARATE

Combination techniques assemble basic techniques into a series which may be used for attack or defence. A combination technique can consist solely of two basic techniques, or a whole series involving kicks, punches and strikes which is either pre-arranged or entirely random. Some combinations use only hand techniques; others use only the feet. A third type combines both hand and foot techniques.

The purpose of combination techniques is to encourage the student to link individual moves in a logical and effective sequence. The tactical fighter will use combinations to trap the opponent. The low reverse punch, for example, diverts the opponent's attention and brings his guard down, opening the head to a back fist.

Single techniques can work if used in the appropriate manner at the correct time. In practice, though, the opponent is more able to identify and deal with a single technique than a whole series coming at different angles to different targets. Combination techniques allow the fighter to sustain an attack, maintaining a relentless pressure on the opponent so he eventually makes a mistake that can be exploited.

When performing a basic technique, the body moves in a way which may favour a particular follow-up technique. For example, a right reverse punch winds the right hip forwards, making a right-footed kick the next logical technique to follow with. The movement from punch to kick is natural and can be accomplished very quickly. The expert karateka instinctively knows which is the correct follow-up to use after each technique and this means he is never caught on the wrong foot.

In basic practice of lunge and reverse punch, the fists are left extended after each blow. This is done to get the novice used to strongly pulling back the non-punching arm which in turn powers the actual punch. In combination practice the techniques are true to life and no punch or kick is left out for the opponent to grab. Each single component of a combination technique must be correctly executed if the next is to succeed. If balance is lost at any stage, the karateka must halt and set himself right before going on with the sequence.

Like basic techniques, combinations are normally performed against the empty air. Therefore, it is necessary to use a punching bag to be able to judge the effects of impact on the sequences practised. It is quite an art to balance techniques against the empty air and quite another to test those same techniques against an actual target. A mirror is another useful training aid for checking the standard and security of techniques used. When using a mirror, the karateka tries to beat his own reflection. A partner provides a target to focus combinations against but care must be taken to control their impacts.

For combination techniques to work in practice, the opponent must really believe that, unless he blocks or moves back, they are going to hit him with a great amount of force. Weak or foreshortened feints will be seen as such and the anticipated defensive response not made.

It is also important to strive for versatility when assembling combination techniques. There is considerable scope for experimentation and the karateka can design those combinations which best suit his particular abilities. Combination techniques must be practised in both advancing and retreating modes since the karateka cannot guarantee he will always be moving in one direction.

Since there are so many permutations of basic techniques, no book could hope to catalogue them all. Therefore a cross-section has been described to provide a base from which the karateka can develop his own.

Combination Hand Techniques

Snap punch/snap punch
This is a useful combination to use when free sparring. The attacker (*tori*) faces his opponent (*uke*) and both are in left fighting stances. Tori closes range until their leading fists are a fist-width apart. He does this by advancing slowly, moving first the left foot a little, then the right. When he is in correct range, he snap punches off the left fist into the side of uke's face. The snap punch is a fast jab with the leading fist, strengthened by a forward lean of the body.

Uke will step back and may try to block the punch but, because it was aimed to the side of his face, his blocking arm will come too far across his own face, causing him to momentarily lose sight of tori. Tori uses this over-blocking to his advantage and, without hesitation, steps quickly forward and snap punches again to the head, this time with the right fist. The length of the advancing step will depend on how far uke stepped back.

For the technique to work, there must be the shortest possible delay between the two punches. The second snap punch must catch uke totally off guard if it is to succeed. The forward lean of the body during the first punch takes weight off the back leg, making it possible to step through quickly.

Reverse punch/reverse punch
This is a similar combination technique to snap punch/snap punch except that it uses two reverse punches in fast sequence. The start is the same, with tori advancing on uke and both in left stances. When distance is correct, tori reverse punches to uke's face with his right fist. The punch must be made strongly and aimed to the side of uke's face. If it is an effective punch, uke may step back and try to block it and, once this happens, tori quickly steps forwards and reverse punches again, this time with his left fist. The second punch is to uke's chest, so there is a tactical variation in the height of targets to be defended.

As before, the two punches must occur in quick succession, otherwise they will be seen as separate individual attacks. The first reverse punch throws weight forward onto the front leg, allowing tori's rear leg to step through quickly. The second reverse punch uses the energy of the moving body, plus the strong pullback of the first punch and, if the timing is correct, it will be just about to impact when the right foot sets firmly down.

Figure 108 Beginning from left fighting stance

Reverse punch/back fist/reverse punch
This very effective combination uses three linked basic techniques in a step-up series of movements. The fast sequencing is almost certain to confuse uke and allow the final reverse punch to succeed. As before, tori and uke face each other in left stance and distance is closed in preparation for the first attack.

Tori pushes forwards with his right leg and only body weight on the leading left leg stops it from sliding forwards. As soon as weight is eased by slightly raising the left foot, this pressure drives the body forward. The extent and speed of forward movement depends both upon the pressure exerted by the back leg and the height to which the left foot is raised. A fast and accurately distanced advance can be achieved with a little practice. It is important to draw up the back leg as the advance is made, otherwise tori's stance will become hopelessly drawn out.

As the left leg is set down, tori reverse punches with his right fist at uke's stomach. At the same time, his left guard is pulled in until it overlies his right shoulder, with the elbow bent and little finger pointing down-

Figure 109 Moving into right cat stance

wards. Uke will move back onto his back leg and attempt to block the punch, or he will actually step back out of range. Without hesitation, the reverse punch is pulled back and the left arm lashes out in a back fist to uke's face. As this extends, tori's right foot is drawn up, to be used again to power the final technique.

Uke has suddenly to switch his attention from a powerful low punch to a swinging back fist at his face. If he has not retreated sufficiently, he will be forced to lean back and bring both hands up to defend his face. As this happens, tori again drives off his right leg and steps forward with the left. As weight comes down, the back fist is abruptly withdrawn in favour of a powerful right reverse punch to uke's chest.

Palm heel block/reverse punch
This combination can be performed equally as well advancing or retreating. It is a response to an attack, countering a blow to the face or body and replying with a reverse punch. It is never a good idea to advance full tilt into a punch and so tori steps from left fighting stance (**figure 108**) into right cat stance (**figure 109**). During the step, he brings back his right arm and wipes it across the front of his body, aiming to catch the punch with palm heel. During this block, the left arm is pulled back with the left fist cocked, palm up, on the hip.

The object of the block is to knock uke's punch to the side, so tori's reverse punch can attack unimpeded. The bent left foot is used to drive the body diagonally forwards and outwards for a left reverse punch (**figure 110**).

The technique can also be used while retreating from an attack. As uke advances and tries a punch or grab, tori steps back from left fighting stance into right cat stance. The distance is short because the attacking punch will be targeted on a precise point and only a few inches of movement are needed to make it miss. During the step back, weight transfers onto the left leg and the right arm wipes across the body, deflecting the attacker's punch. Tori then reverse punches with a forward movement off the back leg. It is important to aim the punch correctly and, if uke has attacked the face, tori should come in under it and attack the chest.

Head block/ridge hand
This is also a combination of block with punch and can be practised while advancing or retreating. From left fighting stance (**figure 111**), tori steps forwards into right forward stance and blocks an attack to the head with jodan uke (**figure 112**, overleaf). Having blocked the blow, the right arm is strongly pulled back and the

Figure 110 Left reverse punch

Figure 111 Beginning from left fighting stance

Figure 112 Stepping into and blocking an attack to the head

Figure 113 Turning the hips and launching a ridge hand strike

energy this generates is used to launch a ridge hand strike to the side of uke's neck or jaw (**figure 113**). Because ridge hand is a circular strike, it is difficult to block and curls around and into the target.

Timing is important with this technique, since the downwards blow must be correctly met and deflected before any follow-up can take place. Range is also important because, unless the descending blow is met at the correct point, it can damage the blocking forearm. The head block must be robust and the body tensed to withstand impact. The ridge hand strike must not be made until the attacking blow is completely nullified.

Combination Foot Techniques

Front kick/roundhouse kick
Front kick/roundhouse kick is one of the simplest foot combinations. It begins in left fighting stance with front kick off the right leg. The kick uses hip-twist to increase range and snap-back to prevent it being grabbed. The guard is held stationary and must not flap about. The right leg sets down on the ball of the foot and immediately the second kick is launched. The right leg swivels and roundhouse kick is snapped out and back again. The second kick uses full hip-twist and is completely retrieved before setting down.

It is also possible to practise this sequence without stepping forward. From left fighting stance, the karateka front kicks with his right foot but returns it back to its original position afterwards. As it settles back, weight is transferred onto it and the posture changes to left cat stance. The following roundhouse kick is then made with the front leg and fighting stance resumed afterwards.

Front kick/side kick
This is quite similar to the preceding combination. A right front kick is delivered from left stance and the guard changes with it. The kick is retrieved and set down, ball of foot first. The left foot is then picked up and brought forward while the supporting leg swivels, turning the body sideways on.

Novices sometimes find that they fail to properly use hip-twist during the side kick. This happens because they have not properly retrieved the front kick and are consequently not poised to continue the sequence.

Roundhouse kick/side kick
This is a more difficult combination technique because it calls for a change in full hip rotation from one direction to another. The right supporting leg has to swivel one way for the left roundhouse kick and then twist back straight again as the foot is set down. The right side kick then causes the left leg to rotate the opposite way. The two kicks are quite different and require different applications since one of them is a straight, thrusting kick while the other is a circular, snapping technique.

The novice may find a great deal of difficulty with this sequence and generally moves too ponderously. The movements must be light and the knees brought quickly to the correct height for each kick. The hips must swivel fully and the kicks extend correctly.

Roundhouse kick/back kick
This is one of the most difficult foot combinations, using a controlled and balanced roundhouse kick to the head to set up a back kick to the groin or mid-section. The roundhouse kick is delivered off the back leg and extended for maximum range, with the upper body leaning back. At full extension, the supporting leg has swivelled around and the body is sideways on.

When the kick is retrieved, there is no attempt to restore the body to a forward-facing posture. Instead, the kicking leg is brought around as the body continues to turn and is set down next to the supporting leg. Weight is transferred onto this leg and the previous supporting leg lifted and driven out in a back kick. The successful combination requires the hips to turn sharply as the roundhouse kick is pulled back. If this is not done, the back will not be square on and the kick will be off centre.

Combination Head and Foot Techniques

Front kick/snap punch
This is the most elementary of the hand/foot combinations. It is a very fast sequence, using the weight of the descending leg to power the snap punch. From left stance (**figure 114**), front kick is made with the right foot and the guard held firmly to the sides (**figure 115**). It is customary to change guard during an advancing kick but that is not done in this instance, since maximum power is the goal. As the kicking leg is pulled back and set down, a great deal of energy is generated and must be harnessed to the punch. Therefore, delivery of the right snap punch is timed so it impacts as full weight descends upon the right leg (**figure 116**).

As the kicking leg is set down, the left hand is forcefully withdrawn and the right fist extended at the same speed. Because the guard has not been changed, the punching fist has a good distance in which to accelerate and is consequently more powerful. Had the guard been changed during the kick, the right fist would have been held forward, giving only half the distance for it to accelerate in. This contrasts with front kick/reverse punch, where it is essential to change the guard during the kick.

Roundhouse kick/reverse punch
This combination uses the natural movement of the hip in the first technique to set up the second. From left fighting stance (**figure 117**), right roundhouse kick swivels the hips and cocks the left fist ready for reverse punch (**figure 118**). It is necessary to keep the arms firmly fixed during the kick, so the punch can accelerate over the maximum distance. The kick is pulled back after delivery and descending body weight used to add power to the punch (**figure 119**). Care must always be taken not to lead with the chin on landing.

Side kick/back kick/back fist
This is a technically difficult sequence relying on the correct execution of each individual part. It begins in left fighting stance (**figure 120**, overleaf) with a side kick delivered from the back leg. The supporting leg swivels until the body is fully sideways on (**figure 121**, overleaf). The kick is retrieved but, instead of turning forwards, the body continues to rotate until the karateka's back is turned to the opponent (**figure 122**, overleaf). The right leg is then set down and weight transferred onto it, providing a stable platform for back kick.

It is important to turn fully after side kick, otherwise the back kick will be off-centre. The novice must avoid just dropping his foot because the action of withdrawal

Figure 114 Beginning from left fighting stance, knees bent and guard maintained

Figure 115 A front kick off the right foot, guard maintained

Figure 116 Snap punch to the face on landing: use pull-back

Figure 117 Left fighting stance in preparation for a right roundhouse kick

Figure 118 Turning the hips into right roundhouse kick

Figure 119 Delivering a reverse punch on landing, as the weight comes forward

provides power for the strong hip-twist needed to set up back kick (**figure 123**). After back kick, the foot drops to the floor a little way behind the supporting leg (**figure 124**) and, as the turn continues, weight is put on the front foot and the leading hand unrolls out into a left back fist to the face (**figure 125**).

Back fist is powered by hip-twist used during the turn forwards and also by the transference of weight forwards over the left leg. As the body rotates to face forwards, the shoulders lag slightly, so a torsion is generated in the spine. The shoulders follow the hips around, releasing the back fist in the last instant. The arm straightens out and is brought sharply back as rotation stops altogether. Back fist must be focused to a target and not allowed to swing widely. Reverse punch can be substituted for back fist if required.

General Comments
It is tempting to perform combinations as quickly as possible and this often happens at the expense of the individual techniques comprising them. At first, the novice should practise a sequence slowly, taking care to make each movement correctly. Only when experience has been gained should the sequence be speeded up.

Each technique must be performed with balance and properly retrieved after use. There is a tendency for beginners to deliver the techniques effectively, but skimp on their retrieval. Since subsequent techniques depend for their success upon a proper set-up, they will progressively deteriorate through a sequence if the standard is not maintained.

When using kicking techniques, it is important that the upper body remains relaxed and the arms move as little as possible. The shoulders must be relaxed, except at the moment of focus. It is also important to maintain a uniform body height throughout a sequence, otherwise the karateka bobs up and down.

Figure 120 Preparing for a side kick from left fighting stance

Figure 121 Side kick from back leg: the body leans away to preserve balance and power

Figure 122 Retrieving the side kick and rotating the body away from the opponent in preparation for back kick

Figure 123 Delivering a back kick, with the heel leading and fists clenched

Figure 124 Turning the body after a back kick, elbow raised for back fist

Figure 125 Back fist to the face with forward body lean

CHAPTER 10: KARATE KATAS

Funakoshi regarded katas as the ultimate form of karate practice. They were designed both to train the athlete and to develop strength and agility. In essence they are series of combination techniques, performed in a regular order and cadence. Unlike combination techniques which are basically linear in direction, katas tend to cover the cardinal points and the karateka learns how to deal quickly with attacks from all directions by imaginary opponents.

There are, broadly speaking, two basic categories of kata, the *shorin* series and the *shorei*. The *shorin* series originates from the *shurite* and *tomarite* schools while *shorei* comes from *nahate*. Although the three towns were close to each other, there were basic differences in that *shurite* appeared more influenced by hard Shaolin wushu and *nahate* by soft Wudang. Accordingly, shorin katas use agility, muscular strength in the upper body and focus in their direct techniques. In contrast, those of the *shorei* depend upon firmly rooted stances, power developed from the *tanden* ('centre of ki energy' or, simply, centre of gravity of the human body) and circular movements.

Shorei and Shorin Katas

The *shorei* series include *sanchin* and *tensho* katas, both of which were originated by Master Chojun Miyagi. Sanchin bears a slight resemblance to the southern Shaolin form known as *samching*. It was designed to build up strength, immovability and the ability to withstand impact, and is therefore a very hard kata characterized by a continuous and dynamic tension of opposing muscle groups. The pitting of antagonistic muscle groups against each other is an ancient system first developed by old wushu Masters. They studied the movements of animals and noticed how they flexed opposing muscles in certain body postures and attitudes. This same analysis was made in America during the twentieth century and resulted in the famous body-building course developed by Charles Atlas.

During sanchin practice, the student is tested by the teacher. The latter uses blows to the student's arms, trunk, legs and groin. Sanchin stance causes the hips to be raised, so the testicles are lifted and made less vulnerable to a low kick. Attempts are also made to push or pull the student off balance to check whether or not he is firmly rooted to the ground. This rooting is vital to the development of power originating from the tanden. Some ryu demonstrate the rigidity of their sanchin by breaking timber spars across the student's body and limbs! Students of other ryu test for sustained muscle tension by holding coins between the cheeks of their backsides and then stepping from stance to stance.

Sanchin involves a prolonged, tremendous tension of the whole body and, because of this, takes a great deal of practice and body conditioning before it can be maintained for any length of time. This tension interferes with normal breathing and some ryu practise *ibuki* (breath control) which is specifically devised to harmonize with it. The karateka breathes in through his nose and forces his diaphragm downwards, so the rib cage expands only a little. Exhalation is through the mouth and is often stertorous. The Uechi ryu practice sanchin without ibuki and rely instead on short, sharp exhalations which produce peaks of muscular contraction throughout the body.

It is impossible to underestimate the role of sanchin kata in traditional karate. Miyagi advocated practising sanchin alone for the first three years of karate training. Properly practised, it both conditions the karateka and teaches him how to develop power correctly. Too many karateka rely entirely upon power generation in the upper body only and, while this is effective, it is never as powerful as that generated in the body's centre of gravity.

Whereas sanchin is very hard, Miyagi's *tensho* kata embodies the principles of softness. Miyagi was undoubtedly quoting from his Chinese mentors when he said that, to master softness, it is first necessary to master hardness. It is claimed that the hard Shaolin wushu schools served only as an introduction to the older, soft Wudang systems. Some wushu historians maintain that, in the Shaolin Temple, the full martial art training of monks began with hard styles and concluded with a study of the soft systems. Only when the Temple was under pressure to train more warrior monks in a short period did the training syllabus halt at the hard-style stage.

It is said that the hard systems are more easily learned in a short time, whereas the soft systems require great aptitude and a lifetime's practice in which to excel. In China today, it is common to use the hard systems as a preliminary training introduction for the *nei chia*. The internal forms themselves are graded according to their degree of advancement with *hsing-ye* (mind boxing) being the most elementary, followed by *pa-kua* and *tai chi chuan* as the culmination of nei chia practice.

Tensho is said to contain all the elements necessary to train the karateka in techniques. Its techniques are circular and seem less obviously forceful than those of sanchin but, since they originate in the tanden, they actually possess a great deal of power. Many modern karateka, sadly, practice tensho without ever understanding its principles.

Seisan is a shorei kata taught widely in the shorin schools. It is something of a bridge between the stolid shorei and the agile shorin, being composed of equal parts of slow, tense movements in the peculiar *hangetsu-dachi* stance and fast, focused techniques. Seisan is also known as *hangetsu* which means 'half moon', the name referring to the semi-circular steps which characterize the first half of the kata. Until 1903, seisan was taught as the first kata but, after that date, it was displaced by the *pinans* (synonym = *heians*). In Japanese karate, little use is made of hangetsu as a training kata to develop power. It is practised in the same way as shorin katas and appears to be tacked to the syllabus as a demonstration rather than a core kata.

Jutte, meaning 'ten hands', is another shorei kata practised in shorin schools. Regular practice of this kata is said to give a karateka the strength of five men. *Jion* kata is named after the famous Buddhist temple Jion-je and is practised in the Shotokan ryu. *Seipai* is practised in Goju ryu and Shito ryu and consists of a number of short-range techniques. *Sanseiriu* is an old Okinawan kata practised by Goju ryu and Uechi ryu.

The most advanced of the shorei series is *suparimpei* and this is one of the few katas to teach concurrent techniques. It is a comparative latecomer to Okinawan karate and was probably introduced from Fukien in the late nineteenth century. The meaning of the name is obscure, though the Chinese characters making it up mean simply 'one hundred and eight'.

The remaining principal shorei katas are *saifa*, *seyunchin*, *shisochin*, *kururunfa* and *naifanchin*. Seyunchin uses short-range techniques, including a sequence where the opponent is seized in a powerful grip and dispatched with spear hand. Naifanchin is a series of three unusual katas in which movement is lateral only. They represent the usage of karate techniques in a situation where it is impossible to step back, perhaps because of the nearness of a wall or cliff edge. Some shorin systems have renamed them *tekki*, which means 'horse riding'. This relates to their dependence upon straddle stance. They are known as *nai hanchi* in the Wado ryu.

As karate training altered to meet the demands of larger classes, some Masters considered it a good idea to devise simple training katas. These were short, easily learned and regular forms, each designed to show particular stances or technique. In the Goju ryu, Miyagi developed two which he named *gekisai dai-ichi* and *gekisai dai-ni*. During the period 1903–1906, Yasutsune Itosu of the shorin school developed five training katas which he called *heians* (peace or tranquility). The heians are also known as *pinans* (peaceful mind) in Okinawa and in the Wado ryu. They were taught to Okinawan schoolchildren when karate was first introduced into the school curriculum. In order of practice, they are heian *shodan*, *nidan*, *sandan*, *yodan* and *godan*.

Heian shodan teaches usage of the back or cat stance, together with knife blocks and augmented forearm blocks. Nidan relies upon forward stance and is simpler in construction and content than shodan. It uses straddle stance and spear hand during the concluding sequences though other shorin schools conclude with knife block. Sandan is shorter than the other heians and uses cat stance and double blocks. It also teaches the elbow block and straddle stance.

An unusual deflection block plus a knee strike is found in yodan and, during its closing sequences, it utilizes a form of knife block which is linked with a grab and pull-down. Godan has some very fast sequences and covers surprisingly little ground. It includes a spectacular leap, followed with a low x-block which is said to be a response to an imaginary assailant armed with a six-foot staff.

Funakoshi devised three still simpler katas which he termed the *taikyokus* ('first cause' or, alternatively, 'great ultimate'). These are no more than series of basic techniques performed in four directions. They are practised within the Shotokan.

The Chinese military attaché to Kume Mura, Kong Shang-Kung, taught a long kata to his students Sakugawa and Yari. It was called *kwanku* which meant a 'look to heaven' but his grateful disciples renamed it *kushanku*, which is the Okinawan reading of his name. Except for in the Wado ryu the kata is nowadays known as *kanku dai*, which means 'contemplating the sky'. The kwanku is the longest kata and is generally taught at brown-belt level of proficiency.

The Chinese military attaché Chinto taught the curious like-named kata known as *chinto* which means 'fighting towards the East'. Funakoshi renamed it *gankaku*, or 'crane on a rock' because of its peculiar one-legged stances. There is no doubt that the kata is derived from a southern variant of *peh hoke* wushu, the 'white crane' school. During the transition from wushu to karate, the characteristic beak-like wushu hand configuration has been replaced by a front fist. Gankaku's stances are fluid and depend upon body movement rather than rigidity for their power. In some schools of karate, gankaku has been re-named chinto.

Rohei kata has many characteristics in common with

chinto, as does *haku-cho* of the Taniha Shito ryu but, in this latter case, more of the original wushu techniques are retained. It appears that several wushu forms are in the process of being converted to karate katas in the present day.

The shorin kata *paqsai*, otherwise known as *passai* or *bassai dai*, has strong and vigorous movements in keeping with the meaning of its name – 'to thrust asunder' or 'to penetrate a fortress'. There are two distinct variants known as *tomari-no bassai* and *matsu-mura-no bassai*. The kata is notable for its usage of the double punch (*yamazuki*).

Wanshu kata was taught by the Chinese martial artist of that name. It includes a series of devastating attacks to the opponent's testicles and responds to attack by an assailant armed with a quarterstaff by wrenching it from his grasp with a spectacular spinning, backwards jump. When the Japanese changed the names of Okinawan katas over to mainland terminology, they lacked a good translation of wanshu and so renamed the kata *empi* (flying swallow) after its swooping attacks. There are two versions of the kata, the longer being practised in the Shotokan school.

Unsu is practised in the Shotokan ryu and is notable for its usage of the one-finger spear thrust. It is also unique among the common katas for its inclusion of prone combat techniques. This area of combat is a general omission from karate techniques as a whole. *Gojushiho* comprises two old shorin katas whose name means 'fifty-four steps'. Practised in the Okinawan capital Shuri, it includes a number of short-range open-handed techniques said to be adapted from the legendary phoenix. *Niseishi* kata, also known as *niju shiho*, incorporates both circular and straight techniques.

Practising the Kata
Kata is more than just a selection of karate techniques. Most katas have some form of practical application, even if at only a low level. When practising kata, it is important to understand the reason for employing a particular technique so it can be performed with meaning and the correct degree of application.

It takes many years for this application to be grasped because, at first, the student is more concerned with what comes next than with its standard. Later, he remembers enough of the kata to be able to concentrate upon the techniques. As he practises yet more, his performance acquires a greater polish but it is only when he can free his mind of the techniques involved that the kata becomes a meaningful and vibrant expression of karate.

The kata is not performed at a uniform speed. There

are pauses, preparation, and flurries of action, just as there would be in a real-life situation. Each imagined attack is anticipated, assessed and then decisively countered, before turning to face a new challenge. Definitive counters are accompanied by kiai and there are seldom more than two per kata. Full power is used in the attacks and, because there is no actual opponent to injure, otherwise dangerous techniques can be employed without concern for an opponent's safety. During kata bunkai, these same techniques must be carefully controlled.

At first, the meanings of some kata techniques may be obscure, and it is only when practising kata bunkai that they can be interpreted correctly. Some techniques simply do not relate to effective defence and are often referred to as the 'hidden techniques'. It has been suggested by some historians that these were originated on Okinawa at a time when the practice of karate was prohibited and are merely frivolous moves designed to prevent the onlooker from understanding the nature of the kata.

Kata competition
A kata competition is a sport form of karate which pits contestants against each other in a display of ability. Of all the forms of competition, it is the most acceptable traditionally, though there are problems when it comes to assessing a performance. Who but a Master of Goju ryu can appreciate the fullest nuances of their seipai kata? Does this mean that each ryu has to be judged by a panel of its own technical officials?

In practice, the judging panel has as wide a spread of knowledge as possible and the judges themselves are highly qualified, mature persons with a long history of karate practice. They may well have a great deal of knowledge of ryu other than their own.

The Federation of All-Japan Karatedo Organizations have sought to regularize its kata competitions by standardizing the way in which each kata may be performed. Therefore the Goju ryu kata *suparimpei* must be performed in the Goju manner only and no style variations are permitted. This is important because, although a particular kata may be found in two or three styles of karate, its performance may well vary significantly from ryu to ryu. A judge who is drawn from one ryu may class these variations as a fault, whereas they are perfectly correct for the school to which the contestant is affiliated.

In order to describe a kata competition, it is best to paraphrase the rules, since they set out in a logical manner the way in which they measure the relative performances of kata. First of all, the kata competition must take place on a flat area surfaced with sprung wood. There is no set size for this area though it should be large enough for the unhindered demonstration of katas.

The judges all wear the same uniform of navy blue blazers, white shirts, official ties, grey trousers and black shoes. The contestants wear clean, white karate suits (*karategi*) on which there is no more than one discreet national badge or number. The karategi must be in a good state of repair and not be ripped or torn. Sleeves must not be rolled up and should come to at least midway between elbow and wrist. The trousers must not be rolled up and should come to no less than midway between the knee and ankle.

There are two types of kata competition, invidivual and team. Individuals consist of males and females competing in their own divisions. Teams consist of three males or three females in their own divisions. The contestants are obliged to perform compulsory (*shitei*) and free (*tokui*) katas, the former being drawn from the following list:

Bassai sho	Bassai Dai	Kanku Sho
Kanku Dai	Gankaku	Hangetsu
Unsu	Seipai	Saifa
Empi	Niju Shiho	Seienchin
Jion	Jitte	Suparimpei
Gojushiho Sho		Gojushiho Dai

The judging panel consists of five judges, one of whom takes control of that particular panel. Each must have a minimum qualification of fourth dan and be above thirty years of age. They normally sit in one line facing the contestants, just in front of the control table, though they may also sit one to each corner of the designated competition area. Each judge has a set of score cards, with whole numbers from one to ten, and decimals in a different colour. The chief judge has a whistle on a lanyard which he uses to call for the judges' score.

The area officials sit on the control table immediately behind the chief judge. They record the name of the kata to be performed and the score received. The scores awarded by the judging panel are noted and the highest and lowest discounted. The middle three are summated and used to assess the kata.

A kata competition consists of three rounds, each one selecting fewer people than the one before. Thus the first round selects sixteen candidates and the second round eight. The last round will decide the winner, second and third places.

There are two types of scoring assessment depending upon the number of areas used per division. If there is only one area, the scores will accrue from round to round but, if two, then the score for each round will stand alone. The accrual of scores means that evenly matched performers can creep ahead over three rounds and ties occur less frequently.

A two area elimination uses two judging panels and there is often a noticeable difference in the level of scores awarded on both. It is for this reason that the two areas each contribute half the numbers for ensuing rounds and, in the single area final, no previous score accruals are taken into account.

The judging panel signifies its score assessment by raising the appropriate cards. The chief judge sounds a sharp blast on his whistle to call for the scores to be displayed and then whistles again to have them lowered. If there is a tie, the contestants' lowest scores are added in. If this fails to resolve the draw, the highest scores are also added. If the tie remains after this, both contestants have to perform another kata of their choice.

When the contestant demonstrates his kata, the panel will look to see whether it is performed with competence and an understanding of its underlying principles. The kata must be technically good, with focus, power, balance and concentration. In addition to this, the panel will look for any other good points upon which to base a score.

If a contestant forgets the kata and comes to a stop, he is immediately disqualified. Similarly, if he varies the kata from its traditional performance, he will be disqualified. Contestants who announce the name of one kata and then perform another are treated as though they have made a mistake in the kata and awarded zero score. Judges must be on the look-out for errors in the kata and these may be signified by a discreet word in the ear of the chief judge.

When they are called by the announcer for that division, the contestants go to the edge of the competition area and perform a standing bow. They then walk to the designated starting point within the area and announce the name of the katas to be performed. In team events, all members perform the same kata at the same time. At the conclusion of the kata, they return to the starting point and stand in ready stance, awaiting the judges' score. Once this has been recorded, they perform a second standing bow and leave the area.

In the first two rounds, contestants may perform any kata from the list as long as they do not do the same ones twice. The third round is completely free and any kata may be performed, whether it is on the list or not.

CHAPTER 11: PRE-ARRANGED SPARRING

Basic Principles

Pre-arranged sparring, or *yakusoku kumite*, is a vital part of the transition from combination techniques to free sparring. It teaches the principles of distance, timing and vigorous application of techniques. Although practice of kata teaches full power applications, it does not instil courage or develop fighting spirit. Like kata, though, it does allow the usage of techniques which are considered too dangerous to use in free sparring (*jiu kumite*). Since the opponent knows what techniques are to be used and what responses must be made, the possibilities of injury arising through misinterpretation are reduced.

Combination techniques are used to initiate an attack or to respond to one. The precise mode of usage is discussed and agreed beforehand. The two karateka will decide in what order each plays the roles of tori and uke before beginning. Either the roles will alternate with each sequence or each partner will keep to the same role for two or three repetitions. For speed of learning, the latter is the best scheme to adopt since it allows mistakes to be corrected while they are remembered. Whichever is selected, both partners must ensure they know what the agreement is.

The attacking partner must make sure he presses home his attack with vigour. Weak techniques are easily brushed aside and give the defender entirely the wrong feel for the sequence. The attack must be on target. When the attacker knows what the defender is going to do, it is tempting for him to tailor his attack to suit the response; if he knows uke is going to knock his arm to the left, he may decide to punch that way a little, so as to aid the deflection. This is bad and must be avoided.

On the other hand, the attacker must not alter his attack to catch the defender at a point where he knows the latter will be vulnerable. For instance, if tori knows that uke is going to respond to his punch by stepping to the right, it is quite wrong of him to redirect the punch in that direction. If uke knows that tori is going to attack with a front kick, it is wrong of him to try and hold on to it. He must always behave as though he had no idea what form the attack is going to take and respond accordingly.

Range is the first thing to sort out before a sequence

is begun. The attack has to be at such a range that, if left unchecked, it would be effective. Beginners often start too far apart, causing blocks and counter-punches to fall short and stances to elongate. The way to measure distance is for the attacker to slide forward a little way on each foot alternately until his front guard is a fist-width from uke's. Once this range is achieved, he should settle himself before launching the attack.

Timing is particularly important in all forms of sparring. When responding to an attack, it is vital to receive as early a warning as possible. In launching the attack, tori has a distinct advantage and, in the small amount of time left to him, uke must identify the attack and take the correct steps to nullify it. The earliest warning of an attack can be seen by watching tori's eyes closely. As tori is about to launch a committed attack, his eyes will momentarily narrow. This reflexive squint is unavoidable and gives early notice that an attack is imminent. It does not occur during feints or uncommitted attacks.

To practise detecting this, partners can use any simple pre-arranged form such as one where tori suddenly launches a powerful straight punch. Uke watches his partner's eyes and, as soon as they narrow, moves quickly to one side. This must be practised slowly before fast sequences are considered. It is possible to respond to a leisurely attack without looking for the eye reflex but fast and powerful attacks are not so easy to deal with.

At first, tori should attack at a speed which allows uke to perform the required response. If uke is successful, tori can slightly increase the speed of his attack so it always tests but does not exceed uke's abilities to cope. An unsympathetic tori can completely demoralize uke by using techniques which are initially too fast and powerful for him.

On the other hand, tori should avoid patronizing uke, especially when the latter is a younger person or a woman. Tori must always treat uke respectfully and as a fellow karateka. Considerate behaviour is the hallmark of the follower of karatedo.

When uke can respond effectively to his attacks, tori should apply them with considerable strength and vigour, in an attempt actually to make them work. Some toris demonstrate their commitment by using a loud kiai during their attack. Before free sparring, yakusoku kumite was the only method of testing techniques and such enthusiasm was put into its practice that injuries were numerous.

Uke must respond to tori's attacks in a realistic manner, treating them as though they are potentially injurious. His response must be crisp and powerful, clearly demonstrating the principles inherent in the sequence being practised. Uke must live the part if he is to progress beyond mere technique.

The procedure is that both partners face each other, approximately 3 metres apart. They perform a standing bow from attention stance and then move into ready stance. The attacker may step forward into his opening stance while the defender steps back. Alternatively, the defender may remain in ready stance, quietly waiting. Tori then moves to the correct range and, after a pause, launches his attack. Uke responds with his counter, using a kiai to identify the decisive technique. When the sequence is concluded, the two karateka separate and resume stances, both clearly demonstrating *zanshin* or awareness of the opponent.

It has been known for an apparently defeated attacker suddenly to revive and defeat the unsuspecting defender. It is for this reason that the defender remains fully alert to the attacker until, by common assent, the sequence concludes. At that time, both partners step back into ready stance. The move is slow and dignified and at no time do they take their eyes off each other. When resuming ready stance, it is important to actually step back and not forwards. This is for the same reason as that previously mentioned. At any time, the attacker could suddenly dart forward and the withdrawal thus serves to keep a safe distance at all times. There is no need for the partners to come to attention stance and bow again until the conclusion of the period of practice.

The Varieties of Pre-arranged Sparring

There are several types of pre-arranged sparring. In *sanbon kumite* (three-step sparring), the attacker will make three successive and identical attacks. The defender will retreat from the first two and counter the third. A typical example would pit a face punch against head block. The attacker steps forward from left stance and aims a *jodan oizuki* to the defender's face. The defender steps back with his left leg into right forward stance and head-blocks the punch. With only the slightest of pauses, the attacker then takes a second step and throws a left lunge punch to the defender's head. The defender steps back into left forward stance and repeats head block. The attacker then attacks a final time with right lunge punch to the head. The defender steps back and head-blocks a third time and then immediately pulls back his head block and delivers a mid-section reverse punch with kiai.

This form of pre-arranged sparring is very good for practising elementary sequences, since it provides several repetitions of blocks and requires repeated timing and constant distancing while moving. It is most often practised in a large class which divides equally into two lines of facing karateka. One side functions as attackers and step forward in unison. At the conclusion of the technique, the roles change and the other side assumes the role of attackers. Afterwards, one karateka at the end of the line runs down to the other end of his line and everyone in that line takes one pace to the right, so they all face new partners. This can be repeated until the original partners face each other again.

There is also a form of pre-arranged sparring using five attacking steps (*gohon kumite*), with the response on the fifth, though this is not used so often these days. One-step sparring (*ippon kumite*) is becoming extremely popular and, as its name implies, one attack is made and meets an immediate counter. This system is used for advanced as well as elementary sequences. Actual free fighting techniques can first be practised in a one-step pre-arranged format and the karateka can assess their value in a free fighting regime.

A single lunge punch attack to the head can be dealt with as well in one step as it can in a three. The attacker merely advances forwards with right oizuki jodan and the defender retreats by stepping back with his left foot and head-blocking (**figure 126**). The punch is knocked, of course, and, immediately this happens, the blocking arm is strongly withdrawn and a mid-section reverse punch used (**figure 127**, overleaf). The two karateka then withdraw and return to attention stance.

Figure 126 Pre-arranged sparring: deflecting a single punch with head block

Figure 127 Pre-arranged sparring: delivering a mid-section reverse punch

An *oizuki chudan* can also be dealt with in a one- or three-step sequence. The attacker and defender both face each other in left forward stances. The attacker steps forward and lunge punches to the defender's chest. The latter withdraws into straddle stance and uses mid-section outer block to divert the punch (**figure 128**). Because the attack is strongly made, the defender must sit firmly into his stance and keep the unused arm to his side.

Using his rear leg like a spring, he then drives forwards, closing range slightly with the attacker. During this move, his unused left arm is pushed across his stomach, only to be sharply withdrawn on landing. The blocking elbow is raised so the forearm is parallel to the ground and, as weight returns to the front foot, it is driven into the attacker's face, using the pull-back of the non-striking arm in increase its power (**figure 129**).

Kicks can also be accommodated within a one- or three-step system and perhaps the most basic is the *suki uke* or 'scooping block' response to a front kick. Both partners begin in the same fighting stances, either both in left or both in right (**figure 130**). The attacker front kicks to the centre of the defender's chest and the latter responds by pivoting on his feet, so his body turns almost completely sideways on, the stance changing to straddle. It is very difficult to land an effective technique upon a spinning target and attempts to do so usually glance off.

The evasion is supported by a right-hand scooping block that curls under the heel and draws the kick upwards and outwards, so the attacker's balance is disturbed (**figure 131**). It is important to break his balance, otherwise he can lash out. The attacker is turned and his foot released so he is forced to drop it inside the defender's. The latter then reverts to a reverse punch stance, using hip-twist to power a gyakuzuki or reverse strike into the attacker's face (**figure 132**, overleaf). The defender then withdraws a full step and remains in fighting stance while the attacker steps diagonally back with his front leg and swivels to once more face his partner.

The second kicking technique uses reverse scooping block to hook the opponent's foot outwards. As before, straddle stance is adopted but, this time, the block curves down under the inside of the attacker's foot (**figure 133**, overleaf) and drops it outside of his own.

Figure 128 Using mid-section block to deflect lunge punch

Figure 129 An elbow strike follows the block

Figure 130 Pre-arranged sparring: both partners in fighting stance

Figure 131 Reverse scooping block hooks opponent's foot outwards

Figure 132 Pre-arranged sparring: a reverse strike into the attacker's face

Figure 133 Reverse scooping block hooks opponent's foot outwards

The defender immediately changes stance from straddle to right reverse punch stance, using the hip-twist to power a mid-section gyakuzuki (**figure 134**). This counter must be used quickly, otherwise the attacker can recover his balance and re-open the attack from a strong position.

In basic pre-arranged sparring, the attacker waits for the defender to reply to his technique and will hold it out for ease of counter. While this is good for basic practice purposes, it is of little use in assessing the value of techniques used in free sparring. In that situation, the opponent does not freeze obligingly into immobility after a single attack. Neither does he leave his arms or legs lying about to be grabbed. Therefore, there is a need to develop a one- or multi-step system which allows practical techniques and responses to be evaluated.

The Wado ryu have developed two additional forms of pre-arranged sparring which tend towards this goal. The first is called *kihon kumite* and it relies upon fast, pre-arranged attacks which are met with effective counters. Some sequences represent a high order of development and feature concurrent movements. The second is *ohyo kumite* and this also involves several attacks and realistic responses. It is more practical for the karateka of lower standards, perhaps, than kihon kumite. The attacks are valid free sparring moves and the responses do not wait upon concessions.

An ohyo kumite can be a fairly long, convoluted

Figure 134 Using hip twist to power a follow-up qyakuzuki

sequence and, done skilfully, it resembles actual free fighting. There is a parallelism here with some of the hard wushu system which use similar training routines in lieu of free sparring. The Japanese fighting art known as *shorinji kempo* also includes long performances of natural-appearing pre-arranged sequences and calls them *embus*. If kihon and ohyo sequences are practised long and hard enough, they lead to the setting up of conditioned responses which are invaluable in rapidly changing situations. The ability to respond correctly without the need for conscious thought is the goal of all true martial artists.

Ju ippon kumite is another variety of advanced pre-arranged sparring limited to single, realistic attacks. The teacher may decide that the attack shall be front kick. He may or may not go on to define the response. If not, then the defender is left free to select one. The attacker then stalks the defender and, at a time and stance of his choosing, launches the set attack. The defender must respond to and nullify it. With more advanced students, the teacher may decide only who is to be the attacker and leave him free to select his own attack sequences. The other partner must function solely as the defender though he may be allowed to pre-empt the attacker if the latter becomes too careless with his guard or distancing.

In the following examples, partners are practising techniques which would work in the competitive area. The techniques which they use are pre-arranged but their mode of usage is as lifelike as possible. From left fighting stance, tori swivels his hips as though to do back kick (**figure 135**). Uke recognizes this and prepares to block that technique but he is mistaken in his assessment. The kick begins to travel straight into the target but, at the halfway point, tori suddenly swivels his hips around and changes the direct back kick into a circling reverse roundhouse. Because uke is anticipating a midsection straight kick, he is completely unprepared for the high turning kick (**figure 136**).

The partners face each other in left fighting stance. Tori front kicks with his right leg and uke pulls back a little, in preparation for reverse scooping block (**figure 137**). The front kick is not what it seems, however, and, as it is halfway extended, tori suddenly swivels on his supporting leg and changes it into a high roundhouse kick (**figure 138**).

Regardless of the type of pre-arranged sparring practised, the underlying theme must be that of cooperation between the partners. They are in no way competing and train together only to perfect their own techniques. If they did not practise pre-arranged sparring, they would not become adept in the techniques they need to master for free-style sparring. They would also revert to their own natural techniques and not try out new sequences which might prove to be valuable.

Figure 135 Pre-arranged sparring: from left fighting stance, tori swivels his hips as though to deliver a back kick

Figure 136 Pre-arranged sparring. The low kick becomes a high turning kick

Figure 137 Pre-arranged sparring: tori appears to front-kick, Uke pulls back

Figure 138 The front kick changes midway into a high roundhouse kick

CHAPTER 12: THE TACTICS OF FREE SPARRING

Free sparring (*jiu kumite*) consists of unprogrammed sparring between partners. Techniques are spontaneous and each partner must use his own initiative in responding to them. Despite this, certain conventions are observed. Dangerous techniques are not permitted and these include open hand attacks to the face, spear hand to the groin, attacks to the joints and direct attacks to the limbs. Techniques must be controlled so that, if they make contact, no injury is caused. The body is better able to absorb impacts and so mid-section techniques are permitted to land with more force. Blows to the head are known to cause brain damage, so only the lightest contact is permitted.

Because of these restrictions, the karate practised in free sparring is not that which would be used in earnest. Funakoshi described how he once beat off an attacker by stepping inside the attack and grasping his testicles. Such an otherwise effective karate technique would not be allowed in free sparring.

Free sparring should not be regarded as the ultimate expression of karate, because it is not. It is merely another form of training; one in which courage, spirit, use of distance, timing and karate techniques are tested in a freer associative format. Despite this obvious reservation, free sparring has been accorded a disproportionate importance, exerting a strong and unbalanced influence on karate's recent development.

Whereas a great deal of karate's more esoteric principles have been poorly grasped – both by the Westerner and the modern-day Japanese-free sparring has been readily accepted as a logical conclusion of the art. In purely practical jutsu terms, it seems rather pointless to practise a fighting discipline without entering into some kind of sparring. As a result of the widespread view, those techniques which are prohibited in free sparring have lost importance whereas those which work therein have received an unfair share of practice and attention.

Funakoshi supported the move to introduce karate to Okinawan middle schools. He believed it would improve the character and moral strength of the pupils. He encouraged the change of *jutsu* to *do* but did not

Figure 139 A powerful knee attack

embrance Kano's theories on free practice (*randori*) which he had taken from the Kito ryu and incorporated in his judo. Funakoshi evidently felt that karate's techniques were inherently more dangerous than those of jiu jitsu and could not be changed to permit a form of sparring with rules. His views were not shared by his disciples.

The Okinawan Master Taira Shinken devised a form of full contact sparring which used kendo armour and boxing gloves but this did not reflect the true nature of karate. Before long, controlled-impact free sparring was unofficially practised in many dojos and, through the years, its practice has become regularized, though there are still variations from dojo to dojo and it is as well to check before sparring with karateka from an unfamiliar ryu. Some prohibit groin contact, others do not. Some allow attacks to the shin and thighs, others do not.

The level of contact also varies tremendously. Some dojos allow heavy body contact while others insist on light contact or none at all. When a technique is clearly successful, it is considered correct for the opponent to acknowledge this by means of a disengagement and a brief nod. If this is done, techniques will remain sharp and effective but, without it, they become scrappy and of little value.

Since free sparring techniques are always controlled to a greater or lesser extent, they will not seriously hurt the opponent. The latter has to appreciate the fact the blow was pulled and react accordingly. It may be that the attacker uses a front kick and, because it is controlled to avoid injury, it travels with less power than it otherwise would have. In this circumstance, the opponent would be expected not to take advantage and grab the leg.

Protective Equipment
Since Shinken's time, there has been a great deal of experimentation with safety equipment. Kendo masks have given way to plastic visors fitted to boxing headgear. Unfortunately, these reduce visibility and tend to mist up in use. While they certainly absorb impact and reduce contusions/lacerations, full power blows to the head still cause brain damage. Gumshields are sensible safety measures since, although contact to the face is theoretically limited, accidents do happen and a properly made and fitted gumshield can save teeth and lips. Proprietary off-the-shelf gumshields are of little value and may even exacerbate injury.

Body armour has been tried but discarded as unwieldy and unnecessary. It is widely felt that karateka should be sufficiently conditioned to withstand a fair degree of impact to the body. Medical assessment of recorded injuries report surprisingly few trunk injuries, even when considerable force is used in sparring.

Breast protectors for women remain a matter of personal choice, since no homologated item of equipment has been designated. While breast protection is a sensible precaution to take, it is advisable only when safe equipment is available. In the absence of such, medical opinion remains divided. If no bra is worn, the breasts can move freely, whereas if one is worn, they can be squashed between the strike and the ribcage, producing trauma.

Adequate groin protection for men is readily available. Boxers' groin guards protect the testicles from the inadvertent but not infrequent injury during free sparring. The plastic cups that slip inside a jock strap should not be used because they can trap portions of the genitalia outside of their protection and cause severe injury on impact. If a groin protector is unavailable, then no underpants should be worn, so the testicles can move on impact and so mitigate injury.

Fist protectors remain a subject of debate. Some take the view that the karateka comes to rely upon their pillowing effect and neglects proper control. If no protectors were worn, the techniques would have to be pulled to avoid causing injury. Medical advice recommends the use of fist protectors with no more than 1 centimetre of padding over the knuckles. This is insufficient to mute impact but reduces local lacerations. The thumb must be left unpadded, otherwise it sticks out and gets caught in eye sockets.

When selecting fist protectors for free sparring, the karateka must check they are safe. He first slips them on and then pulls his hand into a front fist. The padding must cover the front of the knuckles and there should be no seam facing forwards. The pad must not rise up over the knuckles during use.

Shin guards are sensible defensive aids but must be of the soft, non-rigid variety. There are two types — those made from a pull-on elastic tube and those which consist of a foam pad held on by velcro straps. The latter is the easier to get on and off. Some shin guards have a foam extension covering the instep. These are comfortable to use and reduce injury but if they are not properly fastened to the feet they can actually cause injury.

Full-contact mitts and gloves are comfortable in use but take a long time to put on and take off. Unless the securing tapes on the boot are taped in, they can fly about and cause injury. All protective equipment should be kept clean and unripped since frayed mitts can cause injury to the eyes.

The Basic Principles of Free Sparring

A great deal of preparation is necessary before free sparring begins. The most important is the standard of the student's karate techniques. There is little point allowing a beginner to free spar until he can perform combination techniques and blocks with a fair degree of competence. Most injuries occur when inexperienced people are allowed to free spar.

The novice should first test his techniques on a punching bag, so he knows they will work without causing self-injury. A mirror is useful because it reveals openings in the guard. The mirror-user should try to see himself through his opponent's eyes and attack the vulnerable points shown up by the mirror. A whole series of combinations must be tried and those which suit the karateka selected for first-line techniques and practised until they become automatic.

The fighting stance must be fluid, allowing the karateka to move rapidly in any direction. It is an unspecialized stance, yielding the maximum options of attack and defence. Postures like cat and back stance are unsuitable because they have only a restricted application. The unspecialized fighting stance is middle to long, with an equal weight distribution. If it is too low, an attacker can get in underneath and push the karateka back out of the area. If it is too long, movements are slowed because of muscle commitment needed to hold the posture over long periods. A properly formed fighting stance allows kicks and punches to be used with equal ease and removes the possibility of a double leg sweep.

The stance is two fist-widths wide. Less than this and it becomes unstable laterally; more and it opens the groin to attack. The karateka does not face the opponent square on, but stands with his body turned 45 degrees away. Not only does this reduce the size of the body target seen by his opponent but it also deploys the rear hand ready for a reverse punch. If the hips turn too far away, this commonly used counter is rendered ineffective.

In a left fighting stance, the left foot is forward and the left hand leads. This hand is held well to the front, where it can intercept attacks at an early stage. It can also be used for attack, since it need travel only a short distance. The right hand is held, open and waiting, on the belt near the centre line.

The position of the fighters relative to each other is important. If both are in left fighting stance, the tactical fighter will position himself so his front foot lies to the outside of his opponent's. He must never let his foot come inside the opponent's front foot. The person on the inside cannot attack in a straight line and must overreach with techniques. The opponent's angle makes it awkward to use a reverse punch and attacks are more difficult to block because they do not come into the defender's centre line. This tactical usage of body positioning is called *line*.

To maximize its chance of success, a front kick should not be aimed at the opponent's centre line, but rather under his arm. Centre-line attacks are easier to block but off-centre attacks need a whole body movement to evade them. The same comments apply to a snap punch to the face. This should be aimed slightly to the side so that, in blocking, the opponent brings his arm too far across and obscures his own vision. In the split second this occurs, a follow-up strike can be delivered with good chance of success. A second tip is to aim mid-section kicks high on the body, since this makes them harder to block.

Front kicks are fast, long-range techniques but can lead to injury. Inadequately pulled-back toes collide with knees, shins and elbows and so, to minimize risk, the karateka should always aim high and then only when a target presents itself. Short-range front kick is an ideal opener and offers the alternatives of further advance or tactical withdrawal. One-step front kick is not a valid technique for free sparring and the karateka is advised to close to the correct range so a step is not required. If distance is suddenly increased by the opponent's inadvertent movement, a slide forward on the supporting leg should correct it. When advancing after a kick, the karateka must take care to drop his foot to the outside of the opponent's.

The karateka should not telegraph roundhouse kick by an obvious circular delivery. The body should lean back during the kick since this extends range and brings the body back from danger. As the kick develops, the kicking knee is brought as quickly as possible across the body to fend off a sudden counter-attack. The guard is held well forwards and a drag on the supporting leg adds both power and additional range to the technique.

In free sparring, roundhouse kick is powered all the way to the target and back. By this means, better control is maintained and there is also the possibility of a second effective kick from the same leg before it is set down. When double kicking, it is far better to kick to mid-section, withdraw and then kick a second time to the head. As the first kick is launched, the supporting leg swivels 75 per cent, leaving 25 per cent available to make the second kick effective. The converse does not work, however. A high kick needs a fair degree of rotation on the supporting leg and, if done first, leaves only a little for the second, which in consequence is too weak.

Front foot roundhouse kicks are very effective

because they travel only a short distance and their curving path makes them difficult to block. They are best used in conjunction with a feint to the opponent's face which momentarily diverts attention. In that instant, the rear foot slides forwards and takes the weight as the front rises into the fend position followed immediately by the kick proper.

Step-up front leg kicks can be used in many ways as long as they begin with a diversionary feint at the opponent's face. A front foot reverse roundhouse, for example, is an excellent technique but care must be taken to step up to the outside of the opponent's front foot, so he is denied an effective counter-attack. Reverse roundhouse is difficult to control and should never be aimed at the face (**figure 140**).

Back kick is a powerful technique but needs a great deal of practice to perform it quickly enough. It is best used in conjunction with a diversion such as reverse punch. Reverse punch swings the punching hip forwards and the back kick is set up by simply continuing this movement. Side kick is excellent for stopping an attacker from rushing in. The front leg is raised and driven out, while the supporting leg drags forward to absorb impact. Unless weight is thrown forwards, the kick can be over-ridden and the karateka pushed to the floor. Side kick is best from short range and particularly when it is inside the attacker's front guard.

The skilled karateka can make a technique seem what it is not and what appears to be a front kick can

Figure 140 Free sparring: reverse roundhouse kick

suddenly change into roundhouse kick if the supporting leg swivels in the last instant. A roundhouse kick can also be changed to front kick by suddenly pulling the body upright and opening out the hips. This abrupt movement can also transform side kick into front kick. Normally these changes are accompanied by a sliding movement of the supporting leg which takes it to the outside of the opponent's front foot. In free sparring, all kicks should remain unspecialized until as late as possible. By this means, their identity is masked until the last possible instant.

Foot sweeps are effective in unbalancing the opponent. There are two types – the leg sweep proper and the hook. The hook, as its name implies, uses the foot to insinuate behind the opponent's ankle, drawing it in the direction it is pointing. Leg sweep is a strike to the opponent's shin or ankle, knocking it in a particular direction. This is best used where there is a weakness in the opponent's stance – if it is too high or there is insufficient side step, if he is advancing and about to put weight down on his leading foot. All these are susceptible to a hook or sweep but a heavier opponent, standing solidly, is not.

The simplest foot sweep uses the rear leg. The karateka's upper body leans away and his supporting leg swivels, bringing the sweeping leg in a low arc. The sole of the foot leads and the big toe is pulled up while the other toes are depressed. The sole strikes to the rear/outside of the opponent's front foot, knocking it in the direction it is pointing. The karateka's sweep is immediately retrieved after use and his guard must be firmly held because the unbalanced opponent may suddenly lash out as he falls. If the sweeping leg is not withdrawn, the karateka can find his opponent has fallen well to the outside of his front leg and is inaccessible to a fast *coup de grâce*. The karateka momentarily hesitates to see the outcome of his sweep and then moves in for a fast concluding technique.

A double foot sweep is a good way of bringing down a stable opponent. Firstly, a rear leg sweep attempts to knock the opponent's leg outwards, causing him to tense his muscles and resist it. The sweep is then quickly retrieved and used to support a second foot sweep in the opposite direction. If this follows quickly enough, it will harness the opponent's resistance to the first sweep and bring him down.

A hook is an opportunist technique, to be used when circumstances make it feasible. Thus, a blocked roundhouse kick landing to the outside of the opponent's front foot can hook it up and outwards. As with the sweep, an effective guard must be maintained and the opponent's leg lifted high, so he tends to fall at the

Figure 141 A free sparring sequence: attacked with side kick off the back leg, the defender twists to evade his opponent . . .

attacker's feet and not roll away into a corner.

In the following example, the opponent has attacked with side kick off the back leg. The defender twists his body sideways to evade the attack and guards his face, moving very little in order to remain close to the opponent (**figure 141**). His left arm grips the attacker's right shoulder and his right comes under the groin. He sweeps the attacker's foot and turns him in the air (**figure 142**) so he lands on his back at the attacker's feet. A reverse punch concludes the sequence (**figure 143**).

Snap punch is one of the fastest hand techniques and can produce an opening for another technique. When travelling directly into the face, it causes a reflex blink of the eyes, allowing a second, quickly following technique to slip in. When snap punching to the face it is all too easy to actually hit the partner so control must be exercised. The follow-up technique to the mid-section needs less control and can be landed solidly.

Back fist has valuable range. If the partners are in opposite fighting stances, front hand back fist will easily out-range reverse punch. It is, however, easily blocked and should be used only in conjunction with another technique, such as reverse punch to mid-section. It is safer to step to the outside of the opponent's front foot when using it.

Reverse punch is the most popular technique of free sparring. To avoid being punched in the face, the reverse

Figure 142 ... his left arm grips the attacker's right shoulder, and a sweep to the attacker's foot having turned him in the air, lands him on his back

Figure 143 ... a reverse punch concludes the sequence

punching karateka must keep a high front guard as he advances. He must turn his hips square on, but no more, otherwise the technique is weakened. If the opponent is standing a little further away, the karateka can simply step forward while holding the same guard. As weight comes down on the new front leg, his forward hand can be used as reverse punch. Reverse punch is also excellent in a defensive mode and can be used with any combination of blocks. The courageous defender can simply dig in with his rear heel and punch the attacker off as he advances.

Free sparring blocks tend to be simple. The front hand interrupts attacks near the source, slapping them to one side with the open hand. The forearm is used to block techniques which have almost reached the chest and also to scoop kicks that have been avoided by concurrent body evasion. The rear hand is sometimes used to block a punch while the front hand simultaneously counter punches. It is also used to catch a front kick during a step back.

Some fighters favour stopping attacks by moving onto them and countering as they are about to be delivered. Others wait until the technique has developed and then respond to it. A third school evades the attack, waits for it to conclude and then responds in the dead time as it is retrieved.

Free Sparring Tactics
At the commencement of free sparring, the teacher will form the class into two lines. Each member of one line performs a standing bow to his partner in the other. The teacher then calls *Hajime* (begin) and sparring commences. The tactical fighter moves easily around the training area, abruptly changing stance, or making as though to advance suddenly. All the while he studies his opponent. During the initial moving around, the karateka should give his opponent a few openings to see how he will react but, while doing so, must be prepared to take the appropriate defensive measures. If as the karateka seems about to advance, his partner digs in and looks ready to counter, then he is a defensive fighter. If, on the other hand, he immediately advances, then clearly he is an attacking fighter.

Defensive fighters are best dealt with by forcing them to come over to the attack and tempting them to respond to feints. Similarly, attacking fighters should be forced onto the defensive, for it is generally the case that attacking fighters have poor defence and defensive fighters poor attacks. If the opponent backs off and looks nervous, the karateka should straight away attack him.

If the opponent seems to favour kicks, then sparring

distance should be closed, so they are difficult to use. If punches are favoured, then he should be made to overextend by sparring at a greater distance. The southpaw is difficult to spar with from orthodox left stance, so the tactical fighter will switch his stance to southpaw to even chances. It is a good idea to adapt flexibly to the opponent rather than remain fixed in response and performance.

General Comments
Free fighting should be approached in a serious and respectful way. At no time should temper or malice intrude. If one partner feels the situation is getting out of hand, unnoticed by the teacher, he should disengage and return to attention stance and perform a standing bow to his partner before withdrawing.

Sparring between different grades can create difficulties. The higher grade must take a well judged mid-line between encouraging the junior and pointing out his weaknesses through successful attacks. The junior must feel there is a point to his sparring and, if he is overwhelmed by the senior's expertise, he becomes quickly disillusioned and loses the spirit that jiu kumite is intended to inculcate. If, on the other hand, the senior is too accommodating, the junior can develop false confidence and poor competence.

Sparring partners of greatly differing weights must proceed with caution. What seems a controlled technique to the heavier partner can be dangerously violent to the lighter opponent. The most important thing is to establish a rapport with one's partner, so there is cooperation rather than competition.

CHAPTER 13: COMPETITION KARATE

For many years a debate has been raging in the collective Japanese martial arts ways (*budo*) over the role of sporting competition in a system whose professed aim is to reach enlightenment by elimination of the ego. It is not primarily a question of the format of competition which causes dissent, but rather whether competition is acceptable at all.

To the Western mind, competition implies a form of striving against another person, with the object of besting them. The sportsman enters a competition with the desire to win, not in the hope of losing. International karate teams represent the honour and prestige of their countries when they compete in a championship. They do their best to win, to defeat their opponents fairly, but defeat them all the same. These sentiments are alien to the concept of the *do*.

To a follower of the way of karate, who wins is immaterial, since the object is solely to defeat oneself. Once the ego is purged, *satori* is achieved and the way to true mastery of karatedo made clear. The fighter competing in the true spirit of the *do* will certainly do his best to win, for not to do so would be dishonest to both himself and his opponent but, to truly succeed in a combat sport, the competitor must have motivation and aggression. Motivation will drive him on when a lesser man gives up the bout as a lost cause. Strongly motivated karateka have retrieved a seemingly impossible situation in the closing seconds and scraped ahead to take the gold medal. The aggressive karateka uses what amounts to controlled anger against his opponent, saying to himself 'I am better than you and I am going to defeat you!' This is surely incompatible with the way! It is not, however, incompatible with karate jutsu which was devised to fulfil a true self-defence role.

It might therefore be supposed that karate competition is based more correctly upon karate jutsu than karatedo. This is not the case however and, though there might be a similarity in attitude between the karate jutsu student and the sport karateka, the actual techniques are vastly different. In fact, followers of karate jutsu resent the damage competition has done to practical karate.

Competition is karate's major public manifestation. Karateka train under a regime in which competition techniques take precedence. The competition karateka does not need to be able to hit hard, since the world's major competition system is based upon light contact only. Therefore, the sport karateka can sacrifice power and effectiveness in the quest for speed. A generation of techniques and their applications has been originated specifically for karate competition and many traditional standards and values have been diminished.

Competition is only a part of karate, just like kata or basic technique. If the true character of karate is to be retained, its followers and the interested public must be educated into understanding that the national champion of a particular competition may be the best sports karateka but is not by implication, the best karateka.

The Development of Karate Competition

Karate competition developed in Japan and one of the earliest pioneers was Hironori Ohtsuka, the founder of Wado ryu. He held a competition in 1936 and contributed towards the establishment of competition. The Shotokan formed itself into the Japan Karate Association and included free sparring into the syllabus for black belt. From free sparring to competition is a small step and a national, all-ryu system was eventually inaugurated.

This depended upon the correct delivery of a valid technique to a scoring area of the opponent's body with a permissible level of force. Early pioneers maintained that an uncontrolled karate technique to a vulnerable target could kill and so they awarded such definitive techniques *ippon* or 'one point'. With the scoring of this one point, the bout was ended since, in real life, the victim would have been killed or severely injured.

This type of competition was known as *shobuippon* (one-point match). It was deadly boring to watch because the competitors were aware that one slip would cost the bout and gave nothing away, biding time and waiting for an opening. With increasing experience, a second category of score was introduced. It was called the *waza-ari* (half point) and was awarded for a scoring technique which fell slightly short of the perfection needed to gain ippon.

The score ceiling for any bout remained ippon but this could now be achieved by a single ippon score, two waza-aris (*awasette ippon*), or a waza-ari followed by ippon. In this last instance, the first waza-ari would be ignored in the final result so as to preserve the score ceiling.

Under pressure from the Europeans, who wanted a more open system of competition, the Japanese instituted a three-ippon system, or *shobusanbon*. They cancelled the waza-ari and slightly lowered the threshold for awarding ippon, apparently realizing that these definitive techniques weren't! They insisted upon total non-contact and would only score techniques which approached within a couple of millimetres of the target. It soon became obvious that with two competitors moving about the area, it was all but impossible to meet this criterion and so it was dropped in favour of 'skin touch'.

Bouts were judged by a referee, an arbitrator whose duty it was to enforce the rules and four corner judges who signalled scores and fouls to the referee by means of flags and whistles. The sheer subjectivity of score assessment led to continuous disagreements between officials and endless conferences, during which time the competition was stopped. In 1980, the Europeans introduced a new set of rules using a referee, a mirror referee and three-point/six half-point bouts. The mirror referee remained opposite the referee throughout the bout and signalled his opinion by agreed gestures.

Discussion was systematically cut down and reliance upon the arbitrator's opinion as to whether a technique scored or not has been abolished. The reintroduction of waza-ari has produced more open and visually exciting bouts since now the competitors can make a mistake yet still go on to win the bout. The concept of a definitive point has been all but scrapped and a scoring technique can now merit either a waza-ari or, if it is extremely good, an ippon. The ippon threshold of visually exciting and technically difficult techniques has been lowered and a full point is awarded even when they are slightly imperfect.

With the institution of these rules, stability has at last been achieved and future work is restricted to the re-drafting of obscure passages to show their meaning more clearly. High technology has come to karate competition in the form of sophisticated scoreboards which not only show each competitor's score, but also his position with regard to penalties and the unexpired time remaining for that bout.

The Current Rules of Karate Competition

Karate competition takes place on flat, square areas with 8-metre sides. This can be varied at the discretion of the tournament organizers in conjunction with the chief referee and it is not uncommon to find 7- and 9-metre squares. The areas are matted, since medical evidence has proven that severe injuries can be caused by competing on solid floors. Traditional matches still take place on sprung wooden floors and, though not as safe as matted areas, they do afford some protection.

The area is marked out with tape, or by different coloured mats. The 8-metre square is surrounded by a further 1-metre 'run-off zone' which is kept clear to allow competitors to overstep without risk to themselves or bystanders. Where two areas are adjacent, the two run-off zones provide a safety separation of 2 metres. A further line is taped 1 metre within the 8-metre square, and this serves to tell the competitor when he is approaching the area perimeter.

Contestants' standing lines are each 1 metre long and situated 1½ metres either side of the area centre. Two further lines, each ½ metre long, are taped down 2 metres either side of the centre and at right angles to the previous pair. These are the standing lines for the referee and judge. The referee stands with his back to the area control table.

The area must be well away from areas of potential danger such as pillars, central heating radiators, low windows and light fittings. If the area is on a stage, there should be at least a 1-metre zone around its perimeter for safety purposes. Spectators should be kept off all safety zones since competitors are often driven off the area at considerable speed. All approaches to the area must be kept clear so the doctor and first aid have direct access.

Competitors must wear a clean white karategi and are only allowed to wear a number or a badge of their country upon it. The sleeves must be rolled down and not be shorter than mid-forearm. The trousers come to midway between the knee and ankle. The tunic must not be torn or in any way scruffy. It is secured by a belt of rank and, additionally, one competitor wears a red belt (*aka*) and the other a white belt (*shiro*). Plain white teeshirts may be worn under the jacket by female competitors only.

Fist protectors are compulsory, shin pads are optional. By agreement between the tournament organizer and chief referee, shin and instep protectors can be allowed. Groin protectors and gumshields are optional. Spectacles are not permitted, though a competitor can wear soft contact lenses on his own responsibility.

Sweat bands are not allowed and neither are earrings, necklaces or rings. Smooth rings which cannot be removed must be taped over. The hair must be clean and cut to a length where it doesn't impede the bout. Long hair must be fastened back with an elastic band since metal clasps and grips are not allowed on safety grounds. Nails must be kept short and the competitor's hygiene maintained at a level acceptable to the referee. The latter can bar anyone who does not, in his opinion, meet these standards.

The refereeing panel also wear a uniform consisting of a navy blue single-breasted blazer with silver buttons, a white shirt and official tie, mid-grey flannels, navy or black socks and black shoes for off the area, black plimsolls for on it. With the agreement of the chief referee, the panel can officiate in shirt sleeves. Female officials are allowed discreet make-up but must not wear jewellery (except for a wedding ring). Wristwatches should not be worn in case they fly off during the bout. The chief referee can bar any official not wearing the official uniform.

The karate tournament may, for example, include a *kumite* (sparring) competition and/or a kata competition. The kata competition will be divided into male and female categories and then into team and individual matches. Each match is further divided into three rounds. The kumite competition is also divided into male (junior and senior) and female categories and then into team and individual matches. The individual match is divided into weight divisions and each division into a series of bouts. Bouts also describe kumite between individual members of opposing teams.

Individual weight divisions are as follows:

Men's Kumite	Women's Kumite
−60 kilos −65 kilos −70 kilos	−53 kilos −60 kilos + 60 kilos
−75 kilos −80 kilos + 80 kilos	
Openweight (seniors only)	

Minimum age for kumite competition is eighteen years and, in the junior male individuals (there is no junior female kumite), competitors must be under twenty-one years old on the day of competition.

A team consists of an odd number of contestants. Usually a male team is comprised of seven, of which five are competitors and two reserves. This number is not fixed and can be varied by the tournament organizer. The reserves can be deployed at the sole discretion of the team manager. Before each match, the official representative of a team hands in a written fighting order specifying the sequence of competitors. If no new fighting order form is submitted for a subsequent match, it will be assumed that the previous order still stands. If an unnotified change is detected, the defaulting team will be disqualified from the team match. Use of a reserve constitutes a change in fighting order and must therefore be notified. There can be no substitution in other than the first round of an individual match.

For a team match to be meaningful, the competing teams must each have a chance of winning. This means that they may compete only if they can field more than the prescribed number of individuals. Therefore at least three of the five fighters of a team are needed if the match is to go ahead. A reasonable time is allowed for competitors in a particular event to present themselves to the area control table. If they have not done so within that time, the decision will be given against them.

In some cases, the chief referee may feel it appropriate to impose a penalty against an entry that contracted to take part in an event and then did not, or which left the event prematurely, without notifying the tournament organizer. Entries which do not register during the time allocated for that purpose at the beginning of a tournament may well be barred from competing.

The referee panel for any match consists of a referee (*shushin*), a judge (*fukushin*) and an arbitrator (*kansa*). In addition, there is a scorekeeper and a timekeeper. The timekeeper records bout time which is set at three minutes for senior male individuals and two minutes for other categories. This can be varied by agreement between the chief referee and the tournament organizer and it is not unusual to have a final bout lasting up to five minutes. The duration of a bout refers only to fighting time and the clock is stopped each time the referee calls 'Yamei' (stop). The timekeeper gives a 30-second warning before the end of each bout. This and the time-up signal are given by a clearly audible signal such as a battery powered bell or a gong.

A competitor can win a bout by scoring three ippons, six waza-aris, or a combination of the two equalling three ippons. He can also win through his opponent's foul, disqualification or renunciation. Two waza-aris comprise one ippon and the latter can be awarded directly for strong techniques which have good form, are correctly timed for maximum effect and accurately distanced. After delivery, the opponent must display awareness of his opponent's potential for further attack (*zanshin*).

A technique slightly deficient in any one of these criteria may still merit an ippon if it was a kick to the head, if it was delivered just as the opponent attacked, if the opponent's attack was deflected and a counter made to his unguarded back, if it was a sweep or throw followed immediately by a valid scoring technique, or if it was a combination of techniques, each of which would have scored in their own right, delivered before the referee called a halt.

The referee panel will always look for ippon scores in the first instance and award waza-aris only in the second instance. In terms of the criteria required before it can be awarded, a waza-ari is almost comparable to an ippon. If a competitor is disqualified, loses by a foul, or renounces the bout, his opponent will be credited with three ippons and awarded the bout.

Attacks must be limited to the head and face, the

neck, chest, abdomen and back. All blows to the abdomen must be on or above the belt. The best way to envisage the scoring areas of the trunk is to imagine wearing a vest. All areas covered by the vest are scoring areas but the tips of the shoulders are not.

An effective technique delivered at the instant of time-up will be scored. The end of the bout is signalled by the timekeeper and, from that point onwards, no scores may be recorded but the bout may continue until stopped by the referee. A technique delivered after time-up or after the referee calls a halt will not be scored and may result in the offender receiving a penalty. No technique can score if the centre of gravity of the competitor delivering it lies outside the competition area. If, however, the competitor does so from within the area, it may score even if the recipient is outside the area at that time, provided the referee has not called for a halt.

Simultaneous scoring techniques by both opponents on each other will not be scored. This is actually quite rare and there is generally a clear first and second in any exchange of techniques but, when it does occur, it is termed *aiuchi*. The referee ensures that both techniques were scores before deciding aiuchi since often one misses, or does not meet the criteria for a score. In this case, it is disallowed and the opponent's technique recognized.

If neither competitor has achieved three ippons at the end of a bout, a victory can still be awarded if one competitor has more ippons and/or waza-aris than his opponent. If they are tied on score, then the competitor who has shown greater fighting spirit and stronger techniques will be awarded the bout. If the tie remains unresolved, a decision can still be based upon the relative superiorities of the fighters' tactics and techniques. Only when the whole situation has been examined, can a draw (*hikiwake*) be awarded.

To decide the outcome of a team match, bout victories are used as the first criterion. If the teams tie on these, the ippons and waza-aris are counted up and the team with the greater number awarded the victory. If the tie continues, a deciding bout is fought between a selected competitor from each team. The selection is done by the team managers. If the bout ties, an extension is fought and the first competitor to score in it is awarded the victory. A first-score-wins extension is known as *enchosen*.

If the tie persists beyond enchosen, two further competitors are selected and so on, until the tie is broken. Enchosen is also used to resolve a tied individual bout but, if it fails, the panel is obliged to arrive at a majority verdict. Since enchosen is only an extension of a bout, any penalty incurred in the bout itself will be carried forward into it.

To make karate competition safer, certain techniques and actions are prohibited. No techniques may make contact, however light, with the throat. For the purpose of WUKO rules, the throat is defined as the front of the neck between the collarbones and the lower jaw, including the windpipe, voice box and the area of the carotid arteries and jugular vein.

The competitor's body can accept a harder blow than his face and, for this reason, levels of permissible contact vary from area to area. 'Glove-touch' contact only is permitted for the face and head though allowance is made for foot techniques since they are not capable of such fine control. The referee will always interpret the rules governing contact in the light of the situation. If aka steps into what would have been a well-controlled face technique from shiro, then aka's contribution to his own injury will be taken into account and the penalty imposed on shiro accordingly mitigated.

Competitors are not allowed to attack each other's joints, groins or insteps. They may attempt a viable leg sweep but may not repeatedly attack the limbs. Eye attacks and open hand strikes to the face are also disallowed. Throwing techniques must allow the opponent to land safely. Those which restrict his breakfalls or roll outs, or those which drop him onto his head or shoulders, are prohibited.

Some techniques cannot be easily controlled. These include axe kick and spinning reverse roundhouse kick. If the karateka shows control, their usage will not be penalized. If they are wild and uncontrolled, then, for the safety of the opponent, the referee will halt the bout and warn the attacker.

The boundary of the competition area must not be crossed by a competitor while the bout is in progress. If aka or shiro steps out, even by the smallest amount, the bout is halted and the offender dealt with. The action of stepping out of the area is known as *jogai*.

If a competitor fighting close to the area boundary delivers a scoring technique, then steps out, jogai may not be given. In this example, the referee will stop the bout immediately after the score and the step out therefore takes place out of bout time. If, on the other hand, the technique is not scored, the referee does not stop the bout, the step out occurs in bout time and is thus jogai. Jogai is not imposed if a competitor is knocked out of the area.

Wrestling and pushing are not allowed and neither are grabbing and holding on. A competitor may be seized and immediately attacked with a scoring technique but the grasp must then be relinquished. A competitor may be penalized for time-wasting if he persistently avoids the attempts of his opponent to engage with him.

It is very important to be aware of the opponent at all times. This is known as *zanshin*. Lack of zanshin (*mubobi*) puts the competitor in danger and can earn a penalty. For example, the competitor who believes he has scored and dances around the area waving his fist in the air is likely to be penalized for mubobi. He is ignoring his opponent's potential and placing himself at risk. Similarly, the competitor can throw his weight into an attack and virtually run onto the opponent's face punches without adequate guard. This too is mubobi and can be penalized.

In recent years, unscrupulous fighters have feigned injury to bring about the cancellation of a scoring technique. For example, the competitor can feign injury following what was, in fact, a well-controlled head kick. If he does this, the kick may not be scored. The experienced referee will try to make an accurate judgement of the impact and, if he thinks the competitor is feigning injury, he can penalize him.

Competitors must treat each other and the refereeing panel with respect; any lack merits an immediate penalty. The competitor's coach and non-fighting associates must also behave properly, otherwise their man may be penalized for their misbehaviour. In serious cases, an entire delegation can be barred from further participation in the tournament.

Karate competition uses an ascending series of penalties for each separate offence. These penalties are imposed by the referee after consultation with the judge. This consultation need not be verbal since there are prescribed gestures which communicate opinions. The lightest penalty that can be imposed is the warning. Warnings are given for the first instances of minor rule infractions or attempts to infringe the rules.

If a minor offence for which a warning has already been given is repeated during a bout, or in an extension to the bout, a waza-ari penalty may be imposed. This penalty is called a *keikoku*. One keikoku may be given for each category of offence and, if the infraction is serious enough, there is no obligation first to give a warning. The referee can directly impose keikoku.

For a further repetition of the same minor offence for which a warning and keikoku have been imposed, a one-point penalty may be imposed. This is called a *hansoku chui*. One hansoku chui can be imposed for each category of offence. If the infraction is serious enough, the referee may impose hansoku chui directly, without first proceeding via the warning and keikoku.

If the offender repeats the minor infraction once

more, he will lose the bout through a foul (*hansoku*). A hansoku raises the opponent's score to three ippons and terminates the bout. The referee is not obliged to proceed through the sequence, warning – keikoku – hansoku-chui – hansoku. He can impose hansoku directly if there has been a major infraction of the rules. If a competitor is dismissed from his bout, he may still compete in other divisions of that tournament.

Very serious offences can merit a disqualification from the tournament. This penalty is called *shikkaku*. When a competitor receives shikkaku, he may not take part in any further events for which he has entered in the tournament. The chief referee takes part in defining the extent of shikkaku since it may be decided to restrict its effect only to the kumite competition of the tournament and allow the offender to participate in kata.

To merit shikkaku, the offender must have behaved in a way which reflects grave discredit upon the sport. He may have persistently disregarded the referee's directions or become so excited as to lose control of himself. The penalty can also be imposed on a competitor who maliciously sets out to injure his opponent, using prohibited techniques and actions in the process.

Injury during a competition is diagnosed by the doctor at the request of the referee. If a competitor has been injured but not through the fault of his opponent, he may feel unable to continue the bout and renounce it in favour of the opponent. Renunciation is known as *kiken* and results in the opponent's score being credited with three ippons. If both competitors are injured through no fault of either, the scores so far awarded will decide the winner. Where there is an equality of points, the referee will decide the winner through *hantei* (decision) on the basis of the given criteria.

If a competitor is declared unfit to fight again in the kumite competition, he must withdraw on pain of disqualification. If any competitor wins a bout through disqualification on the grounds of inflicting injury, that injured competitor may not fight again in the kumite competition without the approval of the official doctor. If he wins a second bout by similar misfortune, he will be immediately withdrawn from further participation in that competition.

The doctor should not be called gratuitously but only when the referee can see that actual injury has been caused. The function of the doctor is to treat the injury and report to the referee on the injured competitor's fitness to continue.

If a team manager or the official representative of a competitor sees an infraction of the rules, he may report the matter to the arbitrator. This report may be written or verbal. A verbal report is only given when the team manager sees what is obviously an administrative error – such as the wrong fighter being called to compete. Any other infractions of the rules by the referee panel must be reported in writing immediately after the incident. Once the next round has begun, it is too late for any corrective action to be taken. Complaints may only be made where there are obvious infractions of the rules by the referee panel. A complaint on other grounds will be rejected.

The role of the chief referee to a tournament is to ensure that the area dimensions and arrangements are correct; to ensure that all necessary facilities are provided for the running of the tournament; to allocate officials to areas; and to arrange for the appointment of a referee commission to oversee the officials' performance. He must also appoint substitute officials and make the final decision on any question of rules' interpretation.

The arbitrator oversees the running of bouts and, when consulted by the referee, may give his opinion on any point. He may not otherwise speak with the referee and judge. If the referee calls for a vote on any issue, the arbitrator may cast one vote. The arbitrator also oversees the scorekeeping and timekeeping and approves the written record of each match or bout.

The referee is in charge of the bout. He is the only member of the panel allowed to make announcements, award points, impose penalties, explain the basis for any opinion he has given and consult with the other members of the panel. He is also allowed to stop the bout when necessary. His responsibility is not merely confined to the area itself but also to the immediate surrounds.

The judge assists the referee and takes part in consultation with him and the arbitrator when requested. The judge signals his opinions on scores and penalties and may exercise a vote on any issue called for by the referee. All discussions between the panel must be strenuously avoided and reliance placed upon use of the prescribed gestures. Neither the chief referee, arbitrator, referee or judge may occupy other positions during the tournament.

At the start of any bout, the referee and judge take up their position on the appropriate standing lines. The arbitrator sits behind the referee at the perimeter of the run-off zone. The referee beckons the competitors forward to take their positions on the standing lines. The competitor on the referee's right side wears a red belt and the one on his left a white belt. Following an exchange of standing bows between the competitors, the referee will call 'Shobu sanbon hajime' and the bout begins.

Immediately he sees a score, the referee will call 'Yamei' and temporarily halt the bout. All parties return to their standing lines and the referee makes the award after consulting with the judge. If a waza-ari is agreed, the referee holds his arm out and low on the side of the successful competitor and announces 'Aka (shiro) waza-ari'. If an ippon is awarded, he signals with his arm above shoulder height and announces 'Aka (shiro) ippon'. He then calls 'Tsuzukete hajime' (start again) and the bout recommences.

When a competitor has scored sanbon, the referee calls 'Yamei' and all parties return to their standing lines. He raises his hand on the side of the winner and announces 'Aka (shiro) no kachi'. The competitors then bow and leave the area. In a tied bout at time-up, the referee calls 'Yamei' and then seeks the judge's opinion before announcing the verdict. When starting an extension to a bout, the referee calls 'Shobu hajime'.

If the referee points at the offender's feet, he is imposing a keikoku; if at his chest, a hansoku chui and, if at his face, a hansoku. Shikkaku is signalled by the referee pointing first to the offender's face and then to the exit of the tournament hall. Jogais are signalled by the referee pointing with his finger to the perimeter line behind the offender. Sometimes the referee will indicate the number of times an offender has committed jogai by lifting the equivalent number of fingers.

Other Rules

The above rules are those used by the World Union of Karatedo Organizations or WUKO. This is the only international governing body for karate and sets the standards for continental and national events. In addition, there are a number of lesser-used alternatives. The Japan Karate Association uses the one ippon with waza-ari and four corner judges.

The Kyokushinkai have instituted a form of full-contact fighting with no weight categories. Fortunately, national federations do use categories, so lighter karateka also have a chance of winning. Oyama feels that WUKO competition is too sports-oriented and has lost the need for toughness and power. His system therefore allows full power kicks, punches and strikes to the body, head and limbs but curiously does not permit face contact. In order to win a bout, one competitor must be knocked to the floor and ties are resolved by comparing the power generated by the competitors in breaking thicknesses of wood. If this also ties, the verdict is given to the lighter man.

The Kyokushinkai competition is certainly tougher than WUKO's but the fact that it doesn't score face attacks produces unlikely stances and fighting distances.

CHAPTER 14: FIT TO FIGHT

No karateka can ever progress if he is too unfit to train properly and so the purpose of this chapter is to suggest ways in which he can increase his level and type of fitness. Once the sheer effort of trying to keep up with the class is abolished, the karateka is free to concentrate on perfecting technique. Training time is valuable and it is not sensible to devote much of this to an exercise programme which can be followed as well outside the dojo.

First of all, what is fit? Fit has been defined as the total dynamic physiological state of the karateka, on a scale ranging from optimal performance to severe debilitation and death. Leading karateka would be found towards the optimal limit of this scale, fluctuating up and down according to their state of training and the presence or absence of illness. Physical fitness is made up of a number of different factors, each of which makes some independent contribution to the whole.

While some are linked, it is possible for a karateka to have a great deal of one fitness component and very little of another. Fitness for karate is not necessarily the same as that required for marathon running or weight lifting. A different mix of components is required, allowing the karateka to gain the greatest benefit from his training. The components of fitness are as follows:

Body Composition

This refers to the proportions of lean body mass and body fat. It is a better indicator than simple body weight as a component of physical fitness since it is possible for a very muscular person to be overweight according to popular height/weight tables, yet still have a relatively small percentage of body weight deposited as fat. Excess fat limits speed of movement, both of the limb and of the entire body.

The fat karateka may be extremely powerful, but his movements will be slower than a leaner colleague of the same weight. In sport karate, excess fat can limit maximum performance. General flexibility work is also impeded by it.

For competition work, the body should be lightly built, with long arms and legs relative to body length. Range confers a distinct advantage. For power karate, the best physique is undoubtedly a pear shape, with weight concentrated at the hips. This means a low centre of gravity and greater stability stances. Power generated by the tanden is increased at the expense of upper body strength.

Aerobic Endurance

This refers to the capacity of the karateka to do prolonged, light work. The cardiovascular system of the aerobically fit karateka is able to transport large volumes of oxygen and glucose (metabolites) to the muscles and efficiently remove the waste products (katabolites). In theory, the aerobic training regime is therefore aimed at raising the sustainable pumping efficiency of the heart and increasing the volume of air that can be effectively processed by the lungs within unit time. In practice, such training involves any activity, such as jogging, cycling or swimming, which can be maintained over long periods.

The extent to which the karateka needs aerobic endurance is governed entirely by his karate needs. The student must be fit enough to take part in basic training and this will demand a reasonable level. The sports karateka needs to compete only for three minutes or so and then at a non-aerobic level and these same comments apply even more vividly to the trained karateka who merely wants to be able to fight effectively. True fights – i.e., not free sparring or competition – are over in seconds, so the need for aerobic endurance is nil.

Nevertheless, aerobic endurance is a valuable platform upon which to build the other components of fitness which are perhaps more relevant to the karateka's needs.

Muscular Endurance

This refers to the capacity of a muscle, or group of muscles, to work continuously at a high level of activity before exhaustion sets in. Because it does not involve the whole body, comparatively little demand is made upon the cardiovascular system and it is therefore quite different from aerobic endurance. Muscular endurance is dependent upon a number of factors, such as the level of activity and the period over which it is sustained, the strength of the muscle(s), its viscosity and the efficiency of its blood supply.

A muscle's endurance limit is set by its capacity to maintain metabolite/katabolite levels at a tolerable level. It needs oxygen to work efficiently and eliminate lactic acid and carbon dioxide. A build-up of lactic acid in the muscles causes fatigue to set in and its work capacity to reduce. Reaction time becomes longer, the muscle stiffens and becomes unable to relax.

The more a muscle performs a movement during training, over the same range, against the same resistance and at the same frequency and speed as is required on the competition area or dojo, the less likely it is to become fatigued in those situations. This improvement is primarily brought about by an increased involvement of functional motor units as a result of the increased work. Motor units are groups of muscle fibres which are enervated by the same nerve and therefore contract together. A muscle is made up of motor units. The more motor units that become involved, the greater the power in that movement. Work increase improves circulation to muscle fibres by bringing more capillaries into play. By this means, more oxygen and glucose are brought in and waste is removed more efficiently.

The karateka therefore continually practises the technique he wants to strengthen by repetition work. The competition karateka may wish to strengthen his reverse punch and he will therefore practise many repetitions. If he competes in non-contact matches, he need only punch at the air or into a light bag, but those who compete in full-contact or knock-down karate should practise punching with great force against the bag.

Flexibility

Flexibility is the range of movement at a joint or joint complex. It is specific to each joint and increased flexibility will allow power to be applied over a greater range of movement. It facilitates maximal exploitation of a karateka's strength and ability. The strength of the associated muscles is closely allied with flexibility. Many karateka can lift their legs to a respectful height, but cannot hold them there.

The range of movement or freedom of a joint is influenced by a number of factors. The major factors are muscles, ligaments and proprioceptors, and the minor factors are tendons, bony structures and adiposity. It is possible to lengthen the joint capsule but only by long and arduous training. The muscles present less of a problem and should be tackled in the first instance.

Proprioceptors are modified muscle cells equipped with a sensory nerve fibre. They provide information to the central nervous system (CNS) about the degree of contraction or extension in a particular muscle. They are found in muscles, tendons and joints and are particularly responsive to sudden stretching or compression. When a muscle begins to stretch beyond its normal length, the proprioceptors detect it and notify the CNS. The CNS responds by contracting the muscle, thereby preventing its further stretch. Unless the limb is regularly stretched beyond its normal limit, there is little point in flexibility training.

Speed
Speed is the time taken to coordinate joint actions, or to transport the whole body through space. The attacking punch must reach its target in the shortest possible time, reducing the opportunity for blocking or evasion. Conversely, the opponent's attack must be recognized and the correct defensive measure applied. Karateka primarily need to increase limb speed and, secondarily, to increase body speed.

Reaction time refers to the time lapse between perception of the stimulus (i.e., the attacker's punch) and the first muscular contraction of the defensive movement. To increase reaction speed, training must simulate reality. The stance will effect the karateka's ability to respond quickly and specialized stances which limit options should be avoided unless used to enhance specific movements.

Strength
Strength is defined as the maximum force which can be exerted by a muscle, or group of muscles, against a resistance. There are several factors influencing muscular strength. A fresh muscle is stronger than a fatigued muscle. The latter is clogged with katabolites and is stiff and resistant to contraction. The number of motor units comprising a muscle will affect its strength. Larger muscles with a greater number of units will produce more power than smaller muscles. The rate at which sensory impulses are transmitted to the muscle, causing it to contract, also contribute.

The speed a fibre contracts will also influence a muscle's strength. Physiologists have found that the human body contains two classes of muscles differentiated by the speed with which they contract under stimulus. Fast-twitch fibres contract quickly and fatigue equally quickly. Slow-twitch fibres respond more slowly but can sustain contraction over a longer period. The relative amounts of each is determined at birth and remains a limiting factor for most karateka.

Slow-twitch fibres are ideal for the marathon runner but not for the sport karateka or weight lifter. Fast-twitch fibres produce a swift strong movement over a short period and are therefore more relevant.

The fitness requirements for an unspecialized karateka can be summarized by the following:

1. A lean but wide-hipped physique with a short body

in relation to the limbs.
2. A fair degree of strength in the limbs and lower trunk.
3. A high degree of speed, primarily of limb movement.
4. Fast reaction times.
5. A reasonable level of aerobic endurance.
6. A reasonable level of muscular endurance.
7. A high degree of flexibility.

The Warm-up and Cool-down
Karate training involves exertion and, to better meet the demands imposed, it is advisable to warm up beforehand. A proper warm-up raises deep muscle temperature, stretches the muscles, ligaments and connective tissues, thus protecting those parts from injury. Increased temperature leads to stronger and faster muscle contractions and decreased viscous resistance in the muscle.

The warm-up gradually increases demand on the cardiovascular system, resulting in decreased discomfort and increased physical efficiency. Although it is unreasonable to suggest that a good warm-up improves skill, it is fair to say that warm-up may help its realization.

The exercises can be related to a karate training format so as simultaneously to achieve warm-up and practise related movements. The warm-up must be of the correct type for karate and should not usually stress the individual doing it. There should be no delay between completion of warm-up and commencement of training.

It is equally important to cool down after karate training. Many changes must be made before the body can return to normal and the cool-down is a way of doing this efficiently and thoroughly. The muscles have been contracting strongly and pumping fluid in and out of their fibres and, once they cease, this fluid can build up and produce muscle oedema. Oedema is accompanied by stiffness, soreness and, in severe cases, muscular cramps. Stiffness can be eased by continuing mild activity involving the active muscles. Hot baths and massage are also efficacious.

A Preparatory Exercise Programme
The purpose of this programme is to ready the karateka for training. He begins warming up the whole body by running or jumping on the spot. Every tenth jump, the knees are lifted to the chest. The warm-up begins slowly and gradually gathers speed as temperature rises. The tempo can increase slightly over twenty burpees. These begin with the karateka standing upright, arms to side and feet slightly open. The karateka drops into a crouch

with his palms flat on the floor. He then shoots his feet out backwards as far as possible and immediately pulls them back under him. Finally he jumps straight into the air, ensuring that both feet clear the ground.

As an alternative to burpees, the karateka starts in the same position and drops into a crouch but then straightens and front kicks high on one leg. He drops back to the crouch and repeats the stand up and kick but this time uses the other leg. Little power is used during the kick but the knee is raised as high as possible.

Twenty press-ups are performed with the back straight and the head looking forward. The hands are closed into fists and the elbows lock straight at the highest point (**figure 144**). At the lowest point, the chest is just brushing the floor (**figure 145**). Most women do not have strong pectoral muscles and find press-ups

Figure 144 A press-up at its highest point

Figure 145 At the lowest point of a press-up, the chest brushes the floor

difficult. They should be allowed to rest their knees on the floor during press-ups.

Alternatively, from a press-up/legs-splayed position, the body is allowed to dip down and forwards. The head and shoulders lift up and forwards while the stomach drops down to the floor. The back is arched and the whole body then moves backwards and up until the arms are locked straight once again.

Sit-ups are valuable exercises for toning up the stomach muscles. They are best performed with the aid of a partner whose role it is to press down on the ankles, stopping the feet from rising. The knees are bent 90 degrees and the karateka lies on his back, hands behind his head (**figure 146**). He raises up, touches his elbows to knees and sinks back again (**figure 147**). As strength is built up and the number of sit-ups increases, the

Figure 146 The starting point for a sit-up

Figure 147 Completing a sit-up

karateka twists his rising body to touch the knees with alternate elbows.

Once the body is warm, flexibility work can begin. This is best tackled in two instalments. At the beginning of training, a short flexibility programme will help the body meet the requirements of training. The major programme should take place after training and just before the cool-down.

The first flexibility session should consist entirely of static stretching. This uses body weight only to stretch the muscles. For example, the karateka sits down and extends his legs out in front (**figure 148**). He keeps them together and ensures the backs of his knees are pressed firmly to the floor. He reaches forward and grasps the balls of his feet or, if he cannot manage that, seizes his ankles. He then lowers his body forwards, making sure his legs remain flat on the floor. Breathing regularly, he tries to bring his chin down to his knees and holds the lowest point for a count of ten or twenty (**figure 149**).

He then opens his legs as wide as possible (**figure 150**) and twists and bends forward to touch each knee with his forehead (**figures 151, 152**). The head can also dip between the splayed legs (**figure 153**). The movement is smooth and unhurried. The proprioceptors can be fooled and stretching improved if, at the lowest position, the stretched muscles are tightened up for a few seconds and then relaxed.

The figure-four stretch involves extending one leg out straight and pulling the other around and behind. The

Figure 148 Static stretching: the karateka sits down and extends his legs in front

Figure 149 Static stretching; the karateka lowers his body forwards and brings his chin down to his knees

Figure 150 In the next exercise he opens his legs as wide as possible

Figure 151 ... and twists and bends forward to touch first the left knee with his forehead ...

Figure 152 ... and then the right knee

Figure 153 ... and finally, the karateka brings his head down and forward to dip between his splayed legs

Figure 154 Static stretching: the karateka touches the forward knee with his head

karateka first touches the forward knee with his head (**figure 154**), then the rear knee (**figure 155**) and finally down the centre (**figure 156**). The lowest point is held for a count of ten. The karateka then rolls onto his stomach, clasping his hands behind his head. He attempts to lift his lower legs and chest as far off the ground as possible.

The second flexibility programme takes place immediately after training. This is more rigorous and may require the assistance of a partner in what is called passive stretching. The partner assists the stretching process by applying power to the various exercises, taking the limb to the limit of stretch and holding it there. If the exercise is being applied correctly, the karateka will feel the stretch in the belly of the muscle and not near the joints. The karateka should keep within the pain barrier, otherwise tissue damage will result and flexibility be reduced. At no time should the partner ever jerk or suddenly press down on a joint.

Specialized Programmes
To increase leg speed, the karateka can run up hills, use leg weights or run in sand or water. Once fatigue is reached the muscles can be rested and the programme switched to running as quickly as possible downhill. Punches can be speeded up by using wrist weights or punching while holding an elastic strap or inner tube, the other end of which is fastened to wall bars.

To increase muscular endurance and strength in the legs, the karateka can use ankle weights while doing high knee raising, bounds for height and distance and

Figure 155 . . . then he touches the rear knee with his head

squat jumps. Press-ups can be supplemented with weights to quickly fatigue the muscles involved in punching and blocking. Karate techniques can also be practised while holding a barbell.

At first, these exercises should be done in sets of thirty, with a short rest between sets. As endurance builds, sets of seventy or eighty repetitions can be practised.

Figure 156 . . . and finally he stretches forward and down the centre

CHAPTER 15: HEALTH AND SAFETY IN THE DOJO

Age is not a bar to practising karate. Young children can be safely taught selected techniques and the discipline of the karate dojo teaches respect and encourages development of physical skills. They are taught different exercises since their bones are developing and the wrong type can lead to injury or even deformity in later life. Older people will also enjoy karate training provided they set their own standards and do not try to keep up with the younger karateka. The person over forty should see a doctor before joining a karate club. Training is arduous and it is as well to identify any health condition which could make training risky.

Epileptics can train as long as the club has a padded floor. Those suffering from the rare grand mal seizures can fall heavily and sustain injury. The more commonly occurring petit mal seizures often do not involve a loss of consciousness and no special precautions are necessary. Diabetics are usually very knowledgeable of their condition and carry sugar around. As soon as symptoms of low blood sugar occur, the karateka can stop and take remedial action. If training is unexpectedly arduous, sugar level can fall, producing unconsciousness. The sufferer can be quickly brought round by giving sugar or lemonade by mouth.

Karate training can be very beneficial for asthmatics; it helps with breathing and can lead to an improvement in general health. Training will allow the asthmatic to tell the difference between normal breathlessness produced by over-exertion and the onset of an attack. The asthmatic should always have medication to hand.

Cardiac sufferers can train provided their doctor knows and has given approval. Some will suffer chest pains if they work too hard and must be excused. A little rest will set matters to right and training can resume as soon as the attack has passed. Certain virus infections can irritate the muscles of the heart and training should be eased while symptoms persist. If this is not done, the heart can be abnormally affected and the karateka suffer what appears to be a heart attack.

Cardiac arrest can occur through a blow on the chest. If the vagus nerve is stimulated, it can depress and, in some cases, actually stop the heart. Sometimes it restarts of its own accord; other times it must be restarted by cardiac massage.

Haemophiliacs may not practise karate. They can bleed uncontrollably after even a minor knock and may require hospital intervention. The teacher must be informed of all health risks in his class. This can be done by means of a questionnaire which new students are required to fill out before training. Once the teacher knows of and accepts a karateka with a health risk, he can monitor his training. The teacher provides a first aid kit and there will be at least one regular member of the club with a current first aid certificate issued by Medimac, Red Cross, or St John Ambulance.

The safe training hall will have a padded or sprung wooden floor. People do fall during karate training and hard floors can cause injury. When mats are used, they should not be overcrowded and should fit closely together, with no spaces between capable of catching toes or wrenching ankles. The training areas should be well away from low windows, light fittings, wall bars, pillars and heating radiators. Unavoidable intrusions must be covered with padding.

Training must, within the limitations of karate practice, aim at limiting risk of injury. Some ryu advocate snapping arms and legs out to their maximum extent and whip-lashing techniques against the natural limits of a joint. Such practices will lead to injury over a period of time. Karateka tend to suffer with both their knee and elbow joints precisely as a result of this habit. It is far better not to kick or punch with full force unless at a target which can absorb the impact. Where no such brake is used, the techniques should be brought to a halt before the limit of joint movement is reached.

The sensible coach will not overstress his students. Excessive loading causes physical breakdown with loss of fitness and a slower rate of learning.

When sparring, students should be matched evenly. Many accidents occur through mis-matching karateka of different size and ability. Injuries, however slight, should be entered in the club accident book and in the karateka's health monitoring card. This is a personal health record carried with the karateka's Martial Arts Commission licence and grading record. The Martial Arts Commission should be notified of all injuries so it can continue to monitor standards of practice.

Any karateka who has been knocked out should not be allowed to spar again for at least six weeks. If he is allowed to spar within that time and suffers a second head injury, the situation can be serious, with long-term effects on physical well-being and work. The brain is a very delicate organ and, when the head is struck hard, it is subjected to shock waves and stresses that damage thousands of nerve cells. These cannot regenerate and, once lost, remain lost for life. Fortunately there is a degree of redundancy and so prolonged effects may not occur until after several head injuries.

The term 'concussion' is used to describe brain damage. The person may be knocked completely out or he may be stunned. In both cases he is unable to respond normally to questions, sights, smells or sounds. If he appears to recover, the teacher will ask him to explain how the injury was caused. His response will indicate whether he is concussed or not. A karateka who is knocked out, comes round and then passes out again may well be suffering from the effects of a ruptured blood vessel bleeding into the skull. Urgent hospital treatment may be required to remedy the situation.

Hard blows to the mid-section can cause internal bleeding. The kidneys are particularly vulnerable and, when damaged, bleed into the ureters, producing blood in the urine. The liver can be damaged by a kick and release bile salts into the blood stream. This imparts a yellow colour to the skin and whites of the eyes known as jaundice. The spleen is a blood reservoir, located on the left side of the abdomen. If it is ruptured, death can result through internal bleeding. Curiously, a ruptured spleen often causes pain to be felt at the tip of the shoulder.

Excessive bleeding diminishes blood volume and leads to shock. A drop in heart rate or reduction in blood supply to the heart can produce the same symptom. The sufferer will fall to the floor as the level of blood supply to the brain falls. Once the sufferer is horizontal, the supply is restored and the karateka may revive.

Blows to the eye occur frequently in karate. Blurred vision may result but this is not significant unless it persists for longer than twenty minutes. Bleeding into the front chamber of the eye can cause complete and irreversible destruction of vision. Sometimes a drop of blood can be seen at the base of the cornea. This confirms the injury and the sufferer should be kept horizontal while an ambulance is summoned.

Fractures are regrettably not uncommon in karate. The toes are most frequently broken through kicking the opponent's knee cap or elbow. The pain can be relieved by alternate immersion in hot and cold water. An ice pack is also efficacious. The injured toe can be taped to an uninjured neighbour and sparring should be avoided for three or four weeks. Fingers should be treated in the same way.

Legal Liabilities and Insurance Cover
The karateka has certain responsibilities to himself and his training partners. He must listen carefully to what

the teacher is explaining and practise only that technique. Any temptation to experiment must be suppressed until the technique is properly mastered. When delivering the technique, control must be exercised to minimize the risk of injury.

Despite the most stringent safeguards, accidents can and do happen and it is essential to have an insurance policy indemnifying third party claims. A personal accident policy is also worthwhile. This covers periods of absence from work as a result of injuries sustained during training. Such a policy includes weekly benefits and a capital sum payable in the event of permanent injury. Both types of policy are incorporated within Martial Arts Commission annual licences (figure 158). These licences are issued to individual karateka belonging to Commission-recognized karate associations.

The Martial Arts Commission

The Martial Arts Commission, or MAC, was formed in January 1977 as a result of meetings between responsible martial artists, representatives of the Department of Environment, Sports Council and Home Office. All were concerned with the standards of martial arts taught to the public and sought to institute a uniform standard of technical competence and social responsibility.

There is no legal requirement to affiliate to the Commission and the groups which have joined are those with a high technical standard and which are socially responsible enough to cooperate for the benefit of the public. The Commission is by far the largest such organization in Britain, with over 80,000 members. It is the only body recognized by the Sports Council and Central Council for Physical Recreation.

The Commission is composed of governing bodies, each responsible for an activity within Britain. Karate is governed in England by the English Karate Council, in Northern Ireland by the Northern Ireland Karate Control Board, in Scotland by the Scottish Karate Board of Control and in Wales by the Welsh Karate Federation. These are the only nationally and internationally recognized governing bodies for karate in Britain and the serious student must ensure he joins and practises only at an MAC-approved club.

For the address of the nearest Martial Arts Commission-approved karate club, write (enclosing an S.A.E.) to: The Martial Arts Commission, 1st Floor Broadway House, 15/16 Deptford Broadway, London SE8 4PE.

CHAPTER 16: JAPANESE TERMINOLOGY

Terminology varies between ryu, but the following will serve as a basic guide to the Japanese terms used in karate. It is by no means a complete guide but does represent the majority of words.

Aiuchi	Simultaneous scores (both disallowed)
Aka	red (belt colour of one contestant)
Ashi barai	leg sweep
Atemi	vital points of the body
Atemi jutsu	techniques used to attack the vital points
Awasette ippon	two waza-aris adding up to one ippon
Bassai	shorin ryu kata
Bo	staff
Bodhidharma	Indian Zen monk (see Daruma and Ta Mo)
Budo	martial arts way
Bujutsu	martial art techniques
Bushi	Japanese warrior of noble birth
Bushido	warrior's moral code
Chinto	shorin ryu kata/Chinese military attaché
Chuan fa	Chinese boxing
Chudan	mid-section
Dachi	stance
Dan	grade within the black belt
Daruma	Japanese name for Bodhidharma
Do	way or path
Dojo	place of the way, training hall
Embu	pre-arranged training sequence of Shorinji kempo
Empi	elbow
Enchosen	extension to a bout
Enpi	shorin kata, known also as 'wanshu'
Fudodachi	immovable stance
Fukushin	judge
Fumikomi	stamping kick
Gankaku	shorin kata, known also as 'chinto'
Gedan	lower
Gedan barai	lower block
Gekisai	Goju ryu training kata
Geri	kick (see also 'keri')
Gi	tunic
Gohon kumite	five-step sparring

Goju ryu	hard/soft way, a style of karate
Gojushiho	shorin kata
Gyakuzuki	reverse punch
Hachijidachi	ready stance
Hai	yes
Hajime	start
Haito	ridge hand
Hangetsu	shorei ryu kata (*see also* 'seishan')
Hangetsudachi	half moon stance
Hanmei	half forward facing
Hansoku	foul
Hansoku chui	warning of foul
Hantei	decision
Heian	training kata (name means peace, *see* 'pinan')
Heisoku	instep
Heisokudachi	heels together attention stance
Hidari	left
Hikiwake	draw
Hiraken	half-open fist
Hiza	knee
Honbu	headquarters of ryu
Ibuki	controlled breathing
Ippon	one point
Ipponken	one-knuckle fist
Ippon kumite	one-step sparring
Ishin ryu	school of karate founded by D Donovan
Isshin ryu	school of karate founded by I Shimabuku
Jion	shorin ryu kata
Jitte	*see* 'jutte'
Jiu jitsu	Japanese system of unarmed combat
Ji yu ippon kumite	semi-free one-step sparring
Ji yu kumite	free sparring
Jodan	upper
Jodan uke	head block
Jogai	outside of area boundary
Ju dachi	free fighting stance
Juji uke	x-block
Junzuki	lunge punch (*see also* 'oizuki')
Jutsu	techniques
Jutte	shorei ryu kata
Kagezuki	hook punch
Kakato	heel
Kakete	linked hands training in Goju ryu
Kakon	chin
Kama	sickle
Kame	stone-filled jar
Kancho	founder
Kanku	shorin ryu kata

Kansa	arbitrator
Kara	Chinese, empty
Karate	China hand, or empty hand
Karatedo	way of the empty hand
Karategi	karate tunic
Karate jutsu	karate techniques
Kata	training pattern
Kata bunkai	application of kata
Keage	high snap (kicks)
Keikoku	half point penalty
Kekomi	thrusting
Kempo	Japanese reading of chuan'fa, boxing
Keri	kick (see 'geri')
Ki	life force
Kiai	harmony of life force; the karate shout
Kibadachi	straddle stance
Kihon	basic techniques
Kiken	renunciation
Kime	focus
Kingeri	groin kick
Kinteki	junior
Kohei	junior
Koken	bent wrist
Kokutsudachi	back stance
Komekami	temple
Kongoken	iron ring
Koshi	ball of foot
Kumite	sparring
Kumiuchi	grappling
Kung fu	colloquial name for wushu
Kururunfa	shorei ryu kata
Ku shanku	alternative name for the kata 'kwanku'
Kyokushinkai	school of karate founded by Oyama
Kyu	coloured belt grade
Kyudo	way of archery
Kyusho	vital points
Maiai	distancing between opponents
Maegeri	front kick
Makiwara	striking post
Manjinosai	a variant of the sai
Mawashigeri	roundhouse kick
Mawashizuki	roundhouse punch
Mawatte	turn
Migi	right
Mikazukigeri	crescent kick
Mokuso	contemplation
Moroashi dachi	semi-forward stance
Morote uke	augmented block
Mubobi	contestant fails to protect himself

Musubi dachi	another name for attention stance
Nahate	Okinawan school of to-de
Naifanchi	shorei ryu kata (*see also* 'tekki')
Naihanchi	synonym for 'naifanchi'
Nanbudo	school of karate founded by Nanbu
Nekoashidachi	cat stance
Nei chia	internal school of wushu
Nijushiho	shorin ryu kata (also known as 'niseishi')
Ninja	one who practises ninjutsu
Ninjutsu	techniques of stealth
Niseishi	alternative name for 'nijushiho'
Nukite	spear hand
Nunchaku	rice flail
Oizuki	lunge punch (*see also* 'junzuki')
Okinawate	'hand of Okinawa'
Pa kua	school of soft wushu
Passai	alternative name for kata 'bassai'
Peh Hoke	school of hard wushu
Pinan	training kata, meaning 'peaceful mind'
Randori	free practice in judo
Rei	bow
Renraku waza	combination technique
Ritsu rei	standing bow
Rochin	short spear
Rokushakubo	six-foot staff
Ryu	school
Sai	short forks
Saifa	shorei ryu kata
Samching	Shaolin training form
Samurai	Japanese warrior
Sanbon kumite	three-step sparring
Sanchin	shorei kata
Sanchindachi	hourglass stance
Sankukai	school of karate founded by Nanbu
Sanseiriu	shorei ryu kata
Satori	enlightenment
Seiken	front fist
Seipai	shorei ryu kata
Seisan	shorei ryu kata
Seishan dachi	alternative name for 'half moon stance'
Seiza	kneeling posture
Sempai	senior
Sensei	teacher
Seyunchin	shorei ryu kata
Shaolin	Buddhist monastery in China
Shihan	Master
Shi'ishi	strength stones
Shikkaku	disqualification
Shikodachi	straddle stance (feet turned outwards)

Shimpan cho	chief referee
Shiro	white
Shisochin	shorei ryu kata
Shitei	compulsory
Shito ryu	school of karate founded by Mabuni
Shizentai	natural stance
Shobu	competition
Shobuippon	one-point competition
Shobusanbon	three-point competition
Shofu	collarbones
Shorei ryu	karate jutsu developed from nahate and tomarite
Shorin ryu	karate jutsu developed from shurite
Shorinji kempo	Japanese quasi-religious fighting system
Shotokai	breakaway from Shotokan
Shotokan	school of karate founded by Funakoshi
Shukokai	organization practising Taniha Shito ryu
Shurite	school of Okinawan to-de
Shushin	referee
Shuto	knife hand
Shuto uke	knife block
Siu Lum	Chinese alternative reading of Shaolin
Sokuto	edge of foot
Soto harai uke	outer sweeping block
Soto uke	outside block
Suigetsu	solar plexus
Suki uke	scooping block
Suruchin	weighted chain
Suparimpei	shorei ryu kata
Tai chi chuan	soft school of wushu
Taijutsu	Japanese form of unarmed combat
Taikyoku	training kata devised by Funakoshi
Tai sabaki	body evasion movements
Taisho	palm heel
Tameshiwari	wood breaking
Ta Mo	Chinese name for Bodhidharma
Tan	barbell
Taniha shitoryu	variant of Shito ryu founded by Tani
Te	hand
Tekki	shorei kata, also known as 'naifanchin'
Tekko	knuckledusters
Tenshin sho	divine intervention
Tensho	shorei kata devised by Chojun Miyagi
Tettsui	hammer fist
Timbei	round shield
To-de	Okinawan fighting art, later known as 'Okinawate'

Tokui	free choice
Tomarite	school of Okinawan to-de
Tonfa	rice grinder handles
Tori	the person who initiates a technique
Tsuzukete	continue
Uchi	inside
Uchi harai uke	inside sweeping block
Uchi uke	inside block
Uechi ryu	school of karate founded by Uechi
Uke	block, or person who responds to a technique
Uraken	back fist
Urazuki	close punch
Ushirogeri	back kick
Wado ryu	school of karate founded by Ohtsuka
Wai chia	external system of wushu
Waza-ari	half point
Wushu	Chinese martial arts
Yakusoku kumite	pre-arranged sparring
Yamazuki	double punch
Yamei	stop
Yawarra	Japanese unarmed combat
Yoi	ready
Yoroi kumiuchi	grappling in armour
Yoko	side
Yokogeri	side kick
Yudansha	black belt holder(s)
Zanshin	awareness of the opponent
Za zen	seated meditation
Zen	Buddhism based upon meditation
Zenkutsudachi	forward stance

BASIC KATAS FOR PRACTICE
Heian Nidan

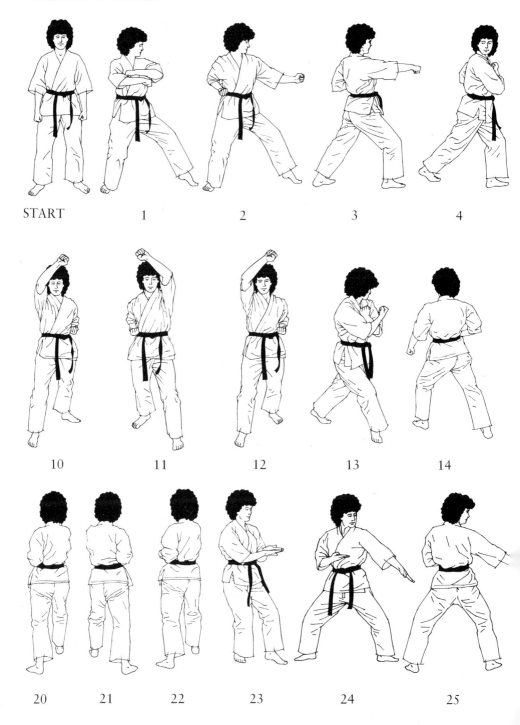

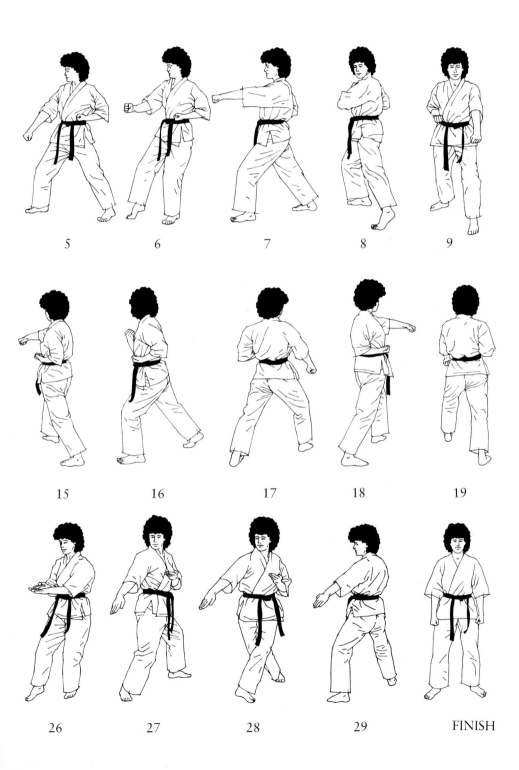

Heian Shodan

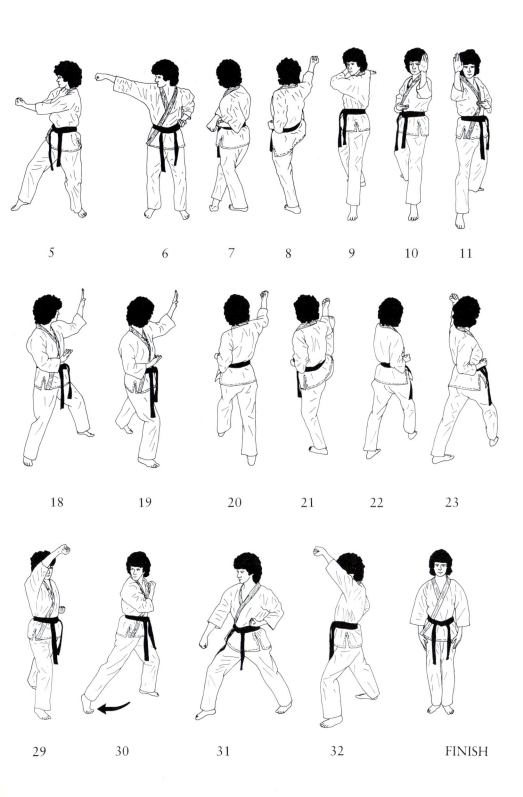

Heian Sandan

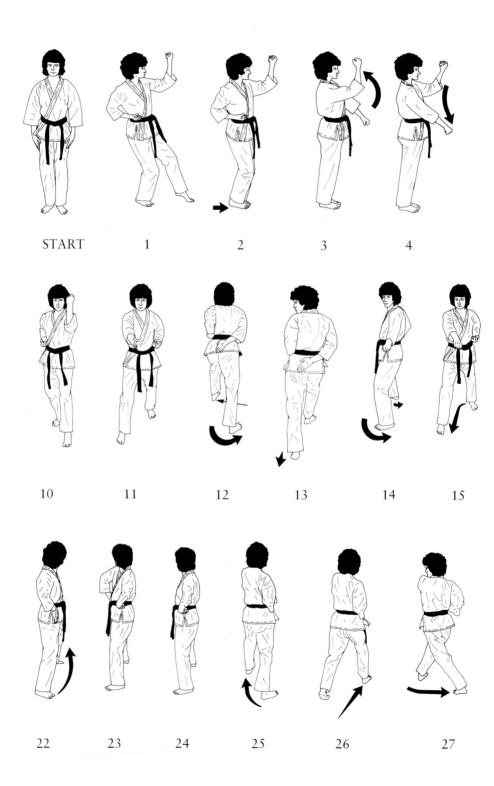

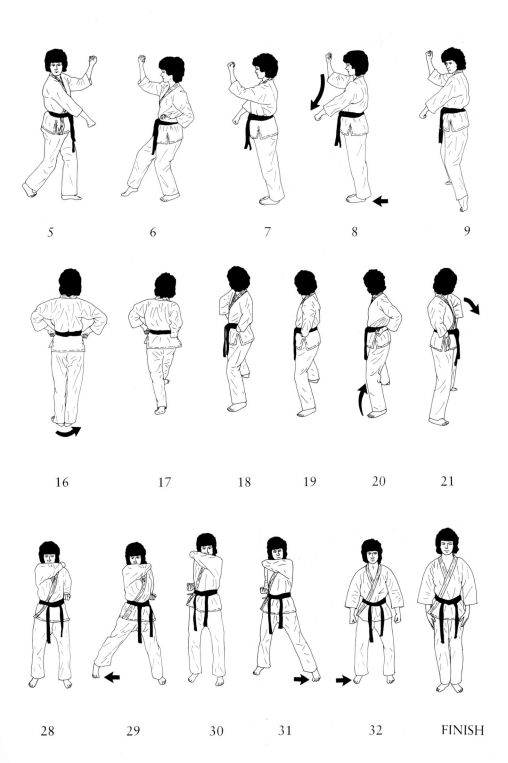

Heian Yodan

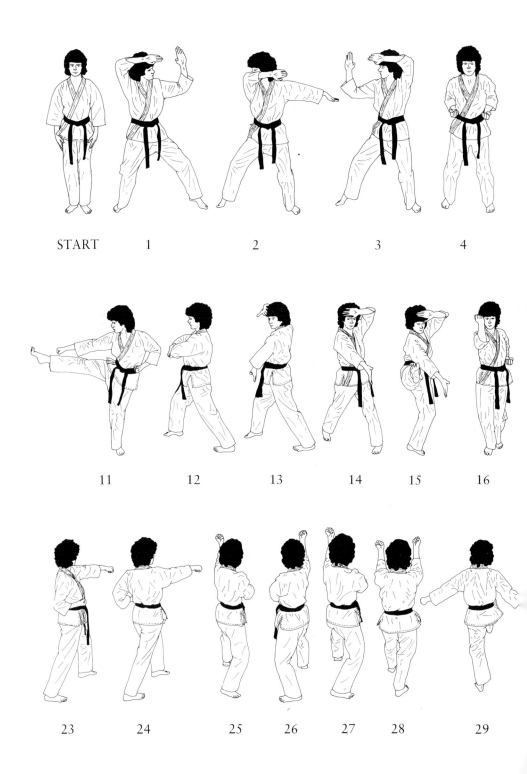

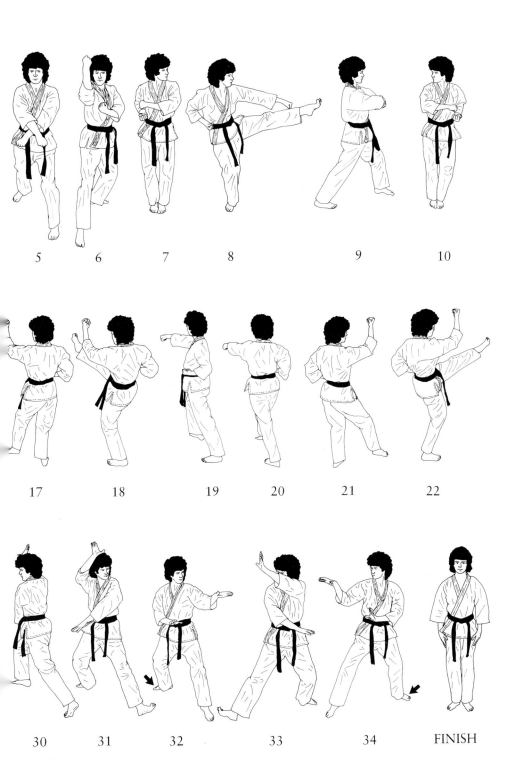

Heian Godan

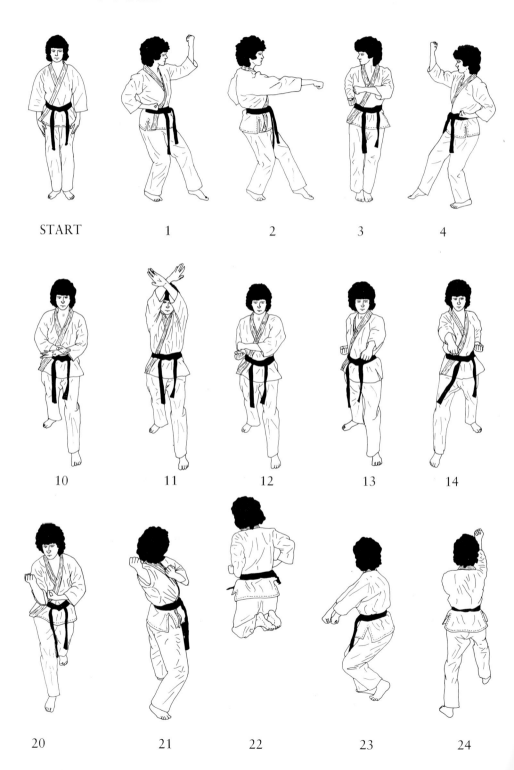

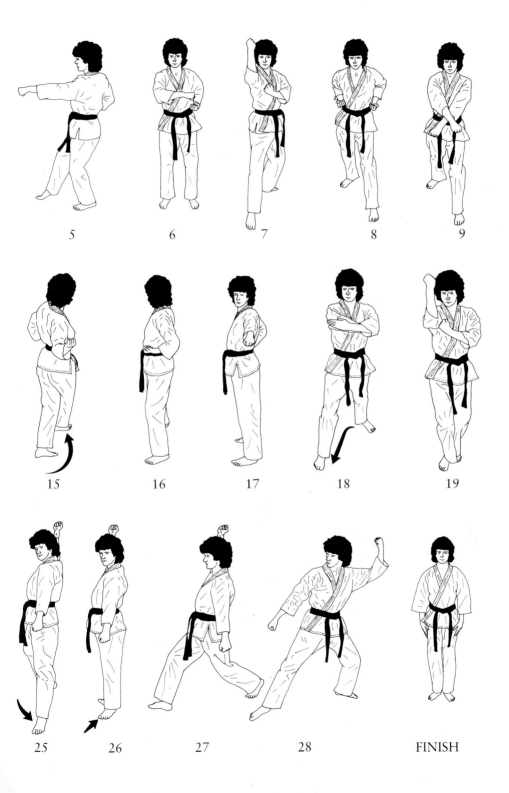

Basai Dai

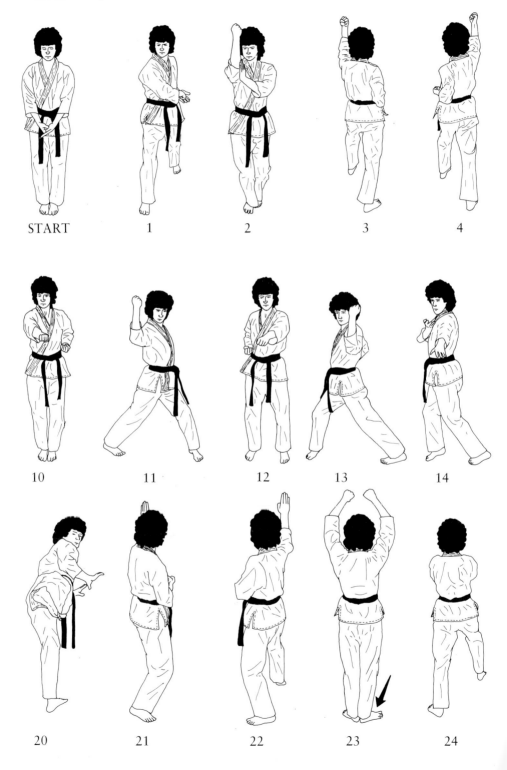

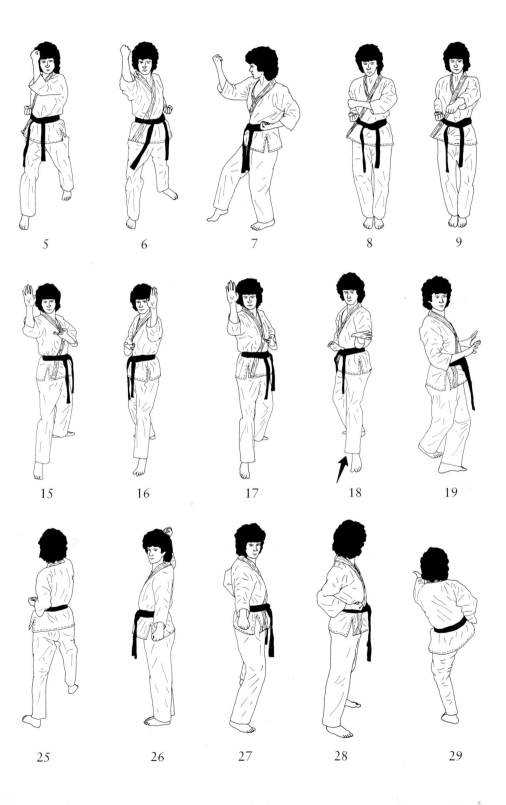

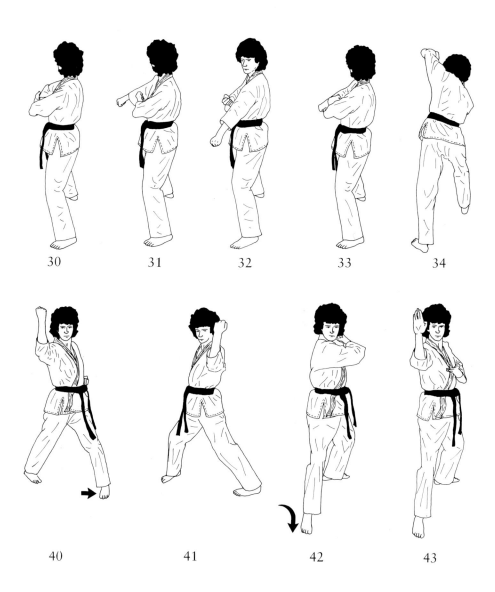

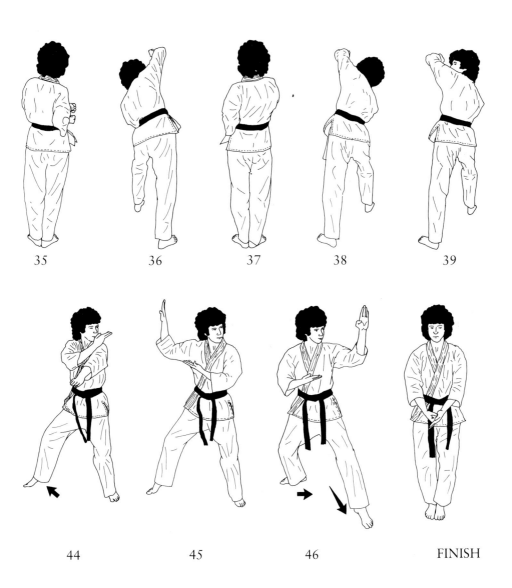

INDEX

aerobic endurance, 155
airbags, 40, 41
arbitrators, 152
arm: augmented forearm block, 72–3; inner block, 71–2, Figs. 52, 53; outer block, 70–1, Figs. 50, 51
asthmatics, 166
attention stance, 42–3, Fig. 7
augmented forearm block, 72–3
axe kick, 63, 149, Figs. 44, 45

back fist, 53–4, 138, Figs. 30, 31
back kick, 63–4, 99–100, 136, Figs. 102–6
back stance, 44, 48, 134, Fig. 10
ball of the foot, 63
basai dai, 186–9
basic techniques, 84–101, Figs. 62–107
belts, 35–7
bleeding, internal, 168
blocks, 67–76, Figs. 50–9; combination techniques, 105–6; free sparring, 140
bo (quarterstaff), 19, 20
Bodhidharma, 8–10, 11
body armour, 132–3
body composition, 154–5
bones, fractures, 168
brain damage, 65, 131, 167–8
breast protectors, 133
breastbone, as target, 66
breath control, 113
burpees, 158–9

cardiac arrest, 166–7
cat stance, 44, 48, 134, Figs. 9, 109
children, 166
chin, as target, 66
chinto kata, 115
circular kicks, 67–8
claw hand, 59–60, Fig. 40
close punch, 80
clothing, 118, 145–6
collarbones, as targets, 66
combination techniques, 38, 102–10, 120, Figs. 108–25
competitions, 39, 142–53; kata, 117–19, 146; sparring, 146
concussion, 168
cooling-down, 158
crescent kick, 64

dan grades, 36–7
deflection blocks, 67–8
diabetics, 166
do, 24–5, 142

dojo, 33–4
Donovan, David, 32

ears, as targets, 65
elbow strikes, 60–2, 124, Figs. 41, 129
epileptics, 166
equipment, 19–21, 39–41, 132–3
etiquette, 33–4
evasion, 67
exercises, preparatory, 158–65, Figs. 144–56
eyes, injuries, 65, 168

Federation of All-Japan Karatedo Organizations (FAJKO), 18–19, 117
feet: combination techniques, 106–10, Figs. 114–25; weapons, 63–4, Fig. 42–7
fighting stance, 47, 134, Figs. 16, 108, 111
fingers: fractures, 168; strengthening, 52
fist protectors, 133, 145
fists: back, 53–4, 138, Figs. 30, 31; combination techniques, 104–5; front, 52–3, Fig. 29; hammer, 55–6, Figs. 33, 34; one-knuckle, 54–5, Fig. 32; semi-open, 56, Fig. 35
fitness, 154–65
five-step sparring, 123
flexibility, 156–7; exercises, 161, Figs. 148–56
floors, safety, 167
focus, developing force, 78, 80
foot sweep, 64, 137, Fig. 142
force, developing, 78–83
forward stance, 46, 48, Figs. 13, 17–19
fractures, 168
free sparring, 120, 131–41, Figs. 139–43
front fist, 52–3, Fig. 29
front kick, 63, 67, 88–92, 135, 136–7, Figs. 42, 74–80
front kick/roundhouse kick, 106–7
front kick/side kick, 107
front kick/snap punch, 108, Figs. 114–16
front-foot roundhouse, 92, Figs. 81–3
Funakoshi, Gichin, 8, 13, 14–15, 16, 18, 19, 25, 28, 30, 112, 115, 131–2

gankaku kata, 38, 115
gekisai dai-ichi kata, 114–15
gekisai dai-ni kata, 115
gloves, protective, 133

Goju ryu, 16, 17, 26–8, 47
gojushiho kata, 116
grade system, 35–7
grip, improving, 52
groin: protection, 133, 145; as target, 66
groin kick, 50
gumshields, 132, 145
gyakuzuki (reverse strike), 125, 126, Figs. 132, 134

haemophiliacs, 167
hair, competition karate, 145
haku-cho kata, 116
half moon stance, 46–7
hammer fist, 55–6, Figs. 33, 34
hands: combination techniques, 103–6, Figs. 108–13; weapons, 52–60, Figs. 29–40
Hanko ryu, 17
hard technique, 78
head: combination techniques, 108–10, Figs. 114–25; injuries, 65–6, 167–8
head block, 68–9, 123, Figs. 49, 126
head block/ridge hand, 105–6, Figs. 111–13
health and safety, 166–9
heart attack, 166–7
heart disease, 166
heel, as a weapon, 63–4, Figs. 44–6
heian godan, 115, 184–5
heian nidan, 115, 176–7
heian sandan, 115, 180–1
heian shodan, 115, 178–9
heian yodan, 115, 182–3
Higaonna, Kannryo, 15–16
high energy punching, 80, 81–2, Fig. 60
high-energy kicking, 82–3, Fig. 61
hook punch, 80
hooks, 137–8
hourglass stance, 47, Fig. 15

ibuki (breath control), 113
immovable stance, 45
injuries, 151, 167; feigning, 150
inner block, 71–2, Figs. 52, 53
inner sweeping block, 76, Figs. 58, 59
inside edge of foot, 64, Fig. 47
instep, 66; protectors, 39, 145; as a weapon, 63, Fig. 43
insurance, 168–9
internal bleeding, 168
ippons, 143–4, 147
Ishin ryu, 32

Japan Karate Association, 143, 153

jaw, as target, 66
jion kata, 114
ju ippon kumite, 127
judges, 118, 119, 144, 145–6, 152–3
jutte kata, 114

kama (sickle), 20, 21
kanku dai kata, 115
karatedo, 23, 25–6, 142
katas, 38, 112–19, 176–89; competitions, 117–19, 146
kiai, 37–8, 80
kicks: combination techniques, 106–10, Figs. 114–25; high-energy, 82–3, Fig. 61; power techniques, 79; pre-arranged sparring, 124; *see also individual kicks*
kidneys, injuries, 66, 168
kihon kumite, 126, 127
Kimura, Shigeru, 29
kinetic energy, 78, 80
knee, as a weapon, 64, Fig. 48
kneecap, as target, 66
kneeling bow, 34, Fig. 4
knife block, 73–4, Figs. 54, 55
knife hand, 58–9, Fig. 38
knuckles, conditioning, 52
kumite competitions, 146, 151
kwanku kata, 115
Kyokushinkai, 19, 32, 153

legal liabilities, 168–9
legs: exercises, 164–5; leg sweeps, 137, Fig. 142
lips, as targets, 66
liver, injury, 168
long-range front kick, 90–1, Figs. 78, 80
lower block, 75–6, 87, Figs. 72, 73
lunge punch, 85–6, 124, Figs. 62–4, 128

Mabuni, Kenwa, 15, 16–17, 29
makiwara (punching post), 39–40, 52
Martial Arts Commission (MAC), 167, 169
meditation, 34, Fig. 5
mid-range front kick, 90, Figs. 74, 75
mirrors, 103, 134
mitts, 39, 133
Miyagi, Chojun, 15–16, 17, 26–8, 35, 67, 112, 113, 114–15
mokuso (kneeling contemplation), 34, Fig. 5
momentum, 79
muscles: endurance, 155–6, 164–5; strength, 157

naifanchin kata, 114
Nanbu, Yoshinao, 32
Nanbudo, 32
natural stance, 43, 48
neck, as target, 66
nei chia, 16, 78, 113
neko-ashi, 42
niseishi kata, 116
nose, as target, 65–6
nunchaku (rice flail), 20, 21

Ohtsuka, Hironori, 19, 28–29, 143
ohyo kumite, 126–7
okinawa, 8, 11–14, 19
one-knuckle fist, 54–5, Fig. 32
one-step side kick, 97, Fig. 96
one-step sparring, 123
outer blocks, 70–1, Figs. 50, 51
outer sweeping block, 76, Figs. 56, 57
Oyama, Masutatsu, 19, 32, 153

palm heel, 56–7, Fig. 36
palm heel block, 75
palm heel block/reverse punch, 105, Figs. 108–10
paqsai kata, 116
passive stretching, 164
physical fitness, 154–65
power development, 78–80
pre-arranged sparring, 120–8, Figs. 126–38
preparatory exercises, 158–65, Figs. 144–56
press-ups, 159–60, 165, Figs. 144, 145
prone combat techniques, 116
protective equipment, 39, 132–3
punches: combination techniques, 103–5; high energy, 80, 81–2, Fig. 60; to increase speed, 164; *see also individual punches*
punching pads, 40–1, 103, 134, Fig. 6
punching posts, 39–40, 52

ready stance, 43, Fig. 8
recoil, 79
referees, 150–3
reverse punch, 81, 86–8, 123, 136, 138–40, Figs. 68–71, 127, 143
reverse punch/back fist/reverse punch, 104–5
reverse punch/reverse punch, 104
reverse punch stance, 46, 48, Figs. 14, 20, 21
reverse roundhouse kick, 100–1, 136, Figs. 107, 140

reverse strike, 125, 126, Figs. 132, 134
ridge hand, 59, Fig. 39
ridge hand block, 75
rohei kata, 115–16
roundhouse kick, 63, 92–5, 135–6, 137, Figs. 81–7; reverse, 100–1, Fig. 107
roundhouse kick/back kick, 107
roundhouse kick/reverse kick, 108, Figs. 117–19
roundhouse kick/side kick, 107
rules, competitions, 144–53
ryu, 26–32

safety, 132–3, 144, 145, 149, 166–9
sai (forked rod), 20–1
sanbon kumite (three-step sparring), 122–3
sanchin katas, 38, 42, 47, 112–13
Sankukai, 32
sanseiriu kata, 114
scissors steps, 90, 95, Figs. 79, 89
scooping block, 124–5, Figs. 131, 133
scoring, 39, 118–19, 143–4, 147–8
seipai kata, 114
seisan kata, 114
semi-forward stance, 45, Fig. 12
semi-open fist, 56, Fig. 35
seyunchin kata, 114
Shaolin monastery, 8–11, 113
Shimabuku, Tatsuo, 32
shin pads, 39, 133, 145
Shinken, Taira, 132
Shito ryu, 17, 29
shock, 168
shorei katas, 112–16
shorin katas, 112–16
short-range front kick, 89–90
short-range power, 83
Shotokai, 19, 31
Shotokan, 30–1, 32, 143
side kick, 63, 83, 95–8, 136, 137, Figs. 46, 91–101, 141
side kick/back kick/back fist, 108–10, Figs. 120–5
sit-ups, 160–1, Figs. 146, 147
snap punch, 135, 138
snap punch/snap punch, 103–4
solar plexus, as target, 66
sparring, 38–9; competitions, 146; five-step, 123; free, 120, 131–41, Figs. 139–43; one-step, 123; pre-arranged, 120–8, Figs. 126–38; safety, 167; three-step, 122–3
spear hand, 57, Fig. 37
speed, 157, 164

spine, as target, 66
spinning reverse roundhouse kick, 149
spleen, injuries, 66, 168
stances, 42–50, 79, Figs. 7–28
standing bow, 33, 43, Fig. 3
static stretching, 161–4, Figs. 148–56
straddle stance, 44–5, 48, 50, Figs. 11, 23–5, 91
strength, 157
stretching, 161–4, Figs. 148–56
strikes: combination techniques, 105–6, Fig. 113; pre-arranged sparring, 124–6, Figs. 129, 132, 134
suparimpei kata, 114
sweeping blocks, 76, Figs. 56–9
taikyokus, 115
targets, 65–6
teams, competitions, 118, 146–7, 148
tensho katas, 112, 113–14
terminology, 170–5
teeth, as targets, 66
temple, blows to, 65
testicles, protection, 133
thighs, as targets, 66
three-step sparring, 122–3
timing, 68, 121
to-de, 8, 12, 13, 19
toes, fractures, 168
tonfa (rice grinder handles), 20, 21
training, 37–9
turn/head block, 86, Figs. 65–7
turning kick, 82–3; *see also* roundhouse kick
turns, 48–50, Figs. 26–8

Uechi, Kanbun, 17
Uechi, Kanei, 17
Uechi ryu, 17, 30, 47
unsu kata, 116
virus infections, 166
visors, 132

Wado ryu, 28–9, 32, 126–7
Wadokai, 19
wai chia, 11, 78
wanshu kata, 116
warm-up exercises, 37, 158
waza-aris, 143, 144, 147
weapons, 19–21; feet, 63–4, Fig. 42–7; hand, 52–60, Figs. 29–40
weight divisions, kumite competitions, 146
women, breast protectors, 133
World Union of Karatedo Organizations (WUKO), 36, 149, 153
wrist: block, 75; as a weapon, 60
wushu, 10, 11, 15, 16, 78, 116

X-block, 70

yakusoku kumite, 38

Zen, 23–6